T0169265

What people are sa

Consciousness and Transcendence

. . . fascinating, very well written, and covers a subject that has always attracted me since childhood.

Arsenio Rodriguez, international development expert, scientist, and poet

Why are you you? In this fascinating book, Loomis Mayer explores the mystery of subjective consciousness, the specific personhood that makes you you. In a lucid and accessible style, Mayer draws on the enormous literature on consciousness — in philosophy, psychology, neuroscience, religion, and art — to probe this greatest of human mysteries.

John Potts, Professor of Media, Macquarie University (Australia), and author of *A History of Charisma* and other books

. . . eloquent and well-reasoned, always rational, but with an emotional core.

Malcolm Jones, writer and editor at *The Daily Beast*, formerly with *Newsweek*; author of *Little Boy Blues*

Consciousness and Transcendence

Art, Religion, and Human Existence

Consciousness and Transcendence

Art, Religion, and Human Existence

Loomis Mayer

IFF
BOOKS

Winchester, UK
Washington, USA

JOHN HUNT PUBLISHING

First published by iff Books, 2022
iff Books is an imprint of John Hunt Publishing Ltd., No. 3 East Street, Alresford,
Hampshire SO24 9EE, UK
office@jhpbooks.com
www.johnhuntpublishing.com
www.iff-books.com

For distributor details and how to order please visit the 'Ordering' section on our website.

Text copyright: Loomis Mayer 2021

ISBN: 978 1 80341 224 5
978 1 80341 225 2 (ebook)
Library of Congress Control Number: 2022911778

A CIP catalogue record for this book is available from the British Library.

Design: Lapiz Digital Services

UK: Printed and bound by CPI Group (UK) Ltd, Croydon, CR0 4YY
Printed in North America by CPI GPS partners

We operate a distinctive and ethical publishing philosophy in
all areas of our business, from our global network of authors to
production and worldwide distribution.

Contents

Prologue ix

Chapter 1: Consciousness and Its Mysteries 1
Chapter 2: Meaning 22
Chapter 3: Beauty and the Arts 31
Chapter 4: Religion 40
Chapter 5: Death 60
Chapter 6: Existence and Transcendence 67

Endnotes 80
A Slightly Annotated Bibliography 91
Name Index 96

Prologue

Why are you *you*? Why are you not *me*? Why are you not a dog? You will say that there are plenty of obvious reasons why you are you, I am me, and Fido (if there are still any dogs named Fido) is a dog. But you'd be wrong. Those reasons only explain why there is a person occupying the place where you're standing. They don't explain why you are experiencing that particular personhood. (Not convinced? Read further!)

Is the nature and origin of subjective consciousness an unsolvable mystery—indeed, a cluster of mysteries? Or can science tell us everything we need to know about it?

For centuries, thinkers have pondered the enigma of mind and body, consciousness and brain, the subjective and the objective. But only in recent decades has the field of "consciousness studies" emerged as a major arena of spirited debate, engaging the concentrated attention not only of philosophers but of scientists in various specialties. With the development of functional magnetic resonance imaging (fMRI) and other techniques, an individual's conscious experience can, at least in a general way, be correlated with the accompanying (and causal?) neurophysiological processes in the brain. But do these correlations actually explain the rise of subjective consciousness, in all of its colorful and emotional glory, from the grey matter of the brain?

I believe that we should follow science as far as it can take us, but this book makes the case that neither science nor theology, neither "physicalism" nor "idealism" nor "panpsychism" (all to be discussed anon), nor anything else can provide full answers. If this makes me a "mysterian," so be it, but it's a position I've reached only after rather careful study of the alternatives. What, then, are we to make of these mysteries? Are there ways in which mystery can be a positive force in our lives and our relationships?

Many other species have powers of vision, hearing, or olfaction that greatly exceed our own. And yet their horizon, unlike ours, does not transcend the bounds of those senses, except perhaps to a limited degree. But the human imagination has virtually no bounds. In fact, we can think about unfathomable things like eternity and infinity, and thus, in the religious imagination, the Absolute.

Given that every human culture has religion, art, music, and storytelling, do these activities have their origin in instinct or in the nature of human consciousness? Is beauty in the eye of the beholder (subjective)? Or are beauty and aesthetic values "out there" (objective)? Or are they, rather, to be found in the relation between "in here" and "out there," between I and Thou?

Various writers, including British neurologist Raymond Tallis, have eloquently and persuasively addressed this question, as well as the nature of human consciousness and our experience of what Tallis—who rejects supernaturalism, as I do—calls "the beyond beyond all beyondering." Throughout this book, I often use such terms as "transcendence" or "the transcendent" to refer to this characteristically human sensibility. Thomas Flynn (*Existentialism*, pp. 69-70) explains Sartre's nonreligious view: "... 'transcendence' denotes primarily the activity of our imagining consciousness by which we reach beyond what we actually perceive to what could or might be perceived." Although many people in many different traditions seek to dissolve their separate selfhood in unity with the transcendent/ the Absolute, I posit, instead, a desire to find ways to *relate* thereto, and to be inspired thereby, without losing one's sense of self. For if there is no *I*, there can be no *Thou*. The origins and roles of both religion and the arts, and of myth and metaphor, can, I will argue, more likely be found in this aspect of human consciousness than in any direct evolutionary adaptiveness.

Many decades ago, when I took an Introduction to Philosophy course in college, I found much that seemed overly abstract, and even today I find much academic philosophical writing tedious and not clearly related to such basic questions as: Why am I here? Why are *we* here? What's it all about? A little later, on my own, I discovered the existentialists, particularly Jean-Paul Sartre and Martin Buber. Despite their obvious differences in thought and style, they spoke, each in his own way, to my condition. I also read with interest many of the books for general readers by the leading psychologists and psychoanalysts. Still later, I became interested in myth and metaphor as they relate to religion and to the human condition, and in recent years I have been exploring the controversies surrounding consciousness and its apparent mysteries. I also have a lifelong interest in the history, theories, and creation of art. In this book I hope to provide something of a synthesis of these themes.

Some friends who started reading earlier, perhaps less well-crafted drafts of this book begged off, saying that they're not trained in philosophy or consciousness studies or whatever. Neither am I, and I've tried to avoid the sort of dry philosophical jargon that has always put me off. If there are terms that are essential to the discussion, I've tried to explain them. This book is aimed at educated general readers interested in joining me in the exploration of the human condition, including consciousness, meaning, the arts, religion and myth, and mystery.

One could say that the central theme of this book is *relation*. As Martin Buber said, "All real living is meeting." The meeting of I and Thou. The meeting of each of us with the yet-to-be-disclosed—with, as Rudolf Otto put it, the wholly other. As I argue in this book, each one of us is wholly other, an I-am-that-I-am. As "it" we are subject to description and comparison, but as "thou" (and in our own "I") we transcend description and comparison. This does not mean that we need to live in separation, in a world of "it," but I argue that we cannot live in total unity, either with individual fellow humans, or with all of humanity, or with nature, or with the Absolute. Rather, as Buber said, if we have both will and grace, we can *meet* the Other, whether a person, a work of art, or an aspect of nature, in all of his/her/their/its singularity, and something new can be disclosed and *lived*.

I thank those who have inspired and encouraged me on this journey, including Cornelia Cotton, Khalid Malik, Arsenio Rodriguez, and most of all my wife, Cary.

Chapter 1

Consciousness and Its Mysteries

The most beautiful experience we can have is the mysterious... the fundamental emotion which stands at the cradle of true art and true science.
Albert Einstein

Once when I was a very small boy, a vivid metaphorical image occurred to me: I saw myself flying around in a little helicopter, and other people were flying around in their little helicopters. We could see each other. We could communicate with each other. But I would never ever be inside anyone else's helicopter, and no one would ever be inside mine. And there was, in my nascent intuition, an arbitrariness to the fact that I found myself in just *this* particular helicopter.

Why am I me, and not you, or anyone else? For that matter, why am I me and not a dog or cat, lion or bird? The great seventeenth-century French philosopher and mathematician Blaise Pascal put it this way: "When I consider the short duration of my life, swallowed up in the eternity before and after... I am terrified, and wonder that I am here rather than there, for there is no reason why here rather than there, or now rather than then."[1] More currently, another French thinker, Michel Bitbol, states the matter thus: "Why am I me, born in this family, this place of the world? ... There were many other possibilities: being any person at any time, or even *not being at all*. And yet here I am, in front of you. Me, not you. Here, not then. ... What is the reason, if any, for this inescapable singularity?"[2]

You may object that I am (and that each of us is) the result of a chain of physical events, including biological evolution on down to the pairing of a particular sperm of my father with a

1

particular ovum of my mother, and then all the events of my life that have shaped my personality. But all of that misses the point. Explaining the objective, observable me—even explaining the fact that I have subjective consciousness—doesn't explain why I am just *here*, experiencing *this* consciousness and no other. Let's put it this way: the objective facts explain why there is a *person* here. They don't explain why *I* am here. Jim Holt, in his bestseller, *Why Does the World Exist?*, observes, with philosopher Thomas Nagel, that all of the objective facts about myself and my origins do not suffice to explain my existence as just this conscious subject, this *me*.[3]

Douglas Hofstadter, well known for his books *Gödel Escher Bach* and *I Am a Strange Loop*, is hardly a "mysterian" regarding consciousness, yet he expresses much the same thought: "Why is this soul in this body? ... Why, when there are so many possibilities, did *this* mind get attached to this body? Why can't my 'I-ness' belong to some other body? It is obviously circular and unsatisfying to say something like 'You are in that body because that was the one made by your parents.' But why were *they* my parents, and not sometwo [*sic*] else?"[4]

In an online article, "Why Am I Me and Not Someone Else?,"[5] Tim Klaassen of Tilburg University in the Netherlands initially appears to agree: "That I am this living self-conscious entity, right here and right now, seems to me one of the most basic facts that I know of. Indeed my very life *consists* in this fact. ... Yet given that there are more self-conscious entities like me out there in the world, it comes to me as rather arbitrary that, of all these self-conscious living entities, I happen to be *this* particular self-conscious entity rather than another. So why am I me rather than someone else?"

Klaassen appears to bolster the argument that this is indeed a central mystery of human existence, extensively citing philosopher Thomas Nagel and pointing out that if my *subjectivity* had been embodied elsewhere than just here, this would change nothing in the *objective* world. But then, at the end, Klaassen asserts that there's no mystery after all: "It seems, then, that the sense of contingency that accompanies the fact that I am Tim Klaassen is *illusory*. Wherever there exists the self-conscious human being that is Tim Klaassen, *I* am necessarily there. ... And that gives my existence a very real and robust quality."

It does not.

In his penultimate paragraph, Klaassen engages in an irrelevant and absurd thought experiment: what if he, having lived for a certain length of time as Tim Klaassen, were to become someone else? But that is not what we're talking about, and it's obviously an absurd impossibility. Obviously, once having been born "Tim Klaassen," he will always be Tim Klaassen (by whatever name) and I will always be Loomis Mayer. An objective causal chain led to his birth and mine, and to our having subjective consciousness. Thus, science can explain the existence of a conscious person named "Tim Klaassen" or "Loomis Mayer" or whoever. But the question remains: Why I am experiencing *this* subjective consciousness, *this* personhood? Physical processes explain why there is a person here, but not why that person is me.

To state the matter yet again: the fact that consciousness is occurring in me (and in you and in everyone else) is caused by the natural chain of cause and effect. Yes, the body is caused, and the consciousness that is a function of the body is caused by the processes of that body and its intersection with the world. But the fact that *I* experience *this* consciousness is uncaused. You will say: "But if it's *your* body, how can your body's consciousness be anything other than *your* consciousness?" To which I must reply: "But why is it *my* body?" To say that it's *my* body because *I* experience it as such puts us into a never-ending circle from which neither science nor reason can extricate us.

Who among us has never said (or thought), upon seeing someone less fortunate than ourselves, "There but for the grace of God go I"? We need not believe in God (and I don't) to reflect that we might have been born rich, talented, and good-looking, or conversely, that we might have been born with physical limitations, or born into an environment of poverty, oppression, violence, fanaticism, and superstition.

We've seen that although all of our physical, psychological, and behavioral characteristics are part of a chain of cause and effect, the fact that I find myself in just this particular body, and in these circumstances, is without discernible cause. It is a gratuitous fact. And even my physical existence, though caused by a physical chain of events, is mysteriously remarkable from the standpoint of probability, when one considers all of the events that had to come together to make this happen. Pascal stated it thus: "I feel that I might not have been, for the 'I' consists in my thought; therefore I, who think, had not been had my mother been killed before I had life. So I am not a necessary being."[6] One could add that I would not exist had a particular sperm cell not united with a particular ovum. As Thomas Nagel (*The View from Nowhere*) has observed, "Amazement that the universe should have come to contain a being with the unique property of being me is a very primitive feeling."[7] And so my physical existence has a gratuitous aspect, even though it results from a causal chain of events; and the fact that *I* experience this existence as *me* is *entirely* gratuitous.

The word "gratuitous" comes from the Latin root *gratia*: "grace," as does the word "gratitude." Can we be grateful even if we don't believe in any sort of conscious deity toward whom we should feel, and express, gratitude? I believe that most of us, except in our darkest hours, do feel, on some level, a sense of gratitude for our fate—a fate that could always have been worse—indeed, we might never have been born.

But the gratuitous aspect of my existence can inspire not only a sense of gratitude but also of anxiety or discomfort. As some existentialist philosophers, notably Sartre, have suggested, my existence as this "I" can be seen as superfluous, as "*de trop*" (basically, needless excess), and in dark hours of depression this sense of *de trop* can overtake us. The existentialists also speak of "thrownness"; we are, as it were, "thrown," without rhyme or reason, into this world.

As a human being, born as the result of a chain of causal factors, and as a subjective consciousness, I live my life in the world, the world of people and things and nature. But as we've seen, my "*am*-ness," my being here and not there, is uncaused. It simply *is*, even though my body, my personality, and my behavior (we will look at "free will" presently) all are a part of a chain of cause and effect. Things—rocks, mountains, rivers, tables, chairs—are caused. Not only things, but processes also—motion, growth, etc.—are caused. Human bodies—and their functions, including consciousness—are caused. But the fact that I am experiencing just this particular embodied consciousness is uncaused. It just *is*.

Kant had a word for that which is uncaused and inaccessible to phenomenal description: *noumenon*. Kant did not invent this word; the ancient Greeks did. The underlying concept is that noumena (plural of noumenon) are "things" that can be thought about but not perceived by the senses. Thus, they are distinguished from *phenomena*, i.e., things and processes that are accessible to our senses. For Kant and, later, for the existentialist philosophers, the issue of the subjective human self as noumenon (uncaused) is bound with the issue of freedom.[8]

Kant recognized the paradox—or antinomy, as he called it—of our experience of self, and of our experience of agency, i.e., free will. He accepted the fundamental principle of modern science, namely, that everything in nature has a cause. Clearly, our bodies are part of the causal chain, along with our bodily processes, including our behavior. But if this is so, how can there be free will? If our behavior is part of nature's causal chain, then we ourselves are not the originators of our behavior, and thus we lack free will. And yet we experience ourselves not merely as objects with various characteristics perceptible to ourselves and to others, but also as subjects, as perceivers of objects, thinkers of thoughts, feelers of feelings—and independent agents of action. Does the human self, then, have some sort of two-fold nature? Was Sartre (who was influenced by Kant) correct in asserting that freedom is the defining characteristic of human existence?

British neurologist Raymond Tallis believes that we do, indeed, have free will. He is not alone in critiquing the Libet experiments, well-known to those who follow the free-will debate. Scientist Benjamin Libet conducted experiments in which people were asked to move their arm whenever they chose to do so. Monitoring of brain activity showed that, about a half-second before the subjects were aware that they had decided to move their arm, the neurological process ("readiness potential") associated with this movement was already underway, thus apparently demolishing the notion of free will—of uncaused free agency.

Libet's research has been critiqued from various angles; Tallis's critique[9] includes the observation that Libet's subjects were engaged in a much larger project than merely moving their arms—starting with their agreement to participate in the experiment and on through all of the actions involved in getting to the laboratory, etc. Thus, the arm-raising occurred not in a gratuitous vacuum but in a larger intentional context. Neuroscientist David Eagleman[10] makes a similar point regarding the contextuality of the Libet experiments. As Tallis indicates, our "will," if it exists, cannot be reduced to the presence or absence of action potentials.

While I heartily agree with Tallis that subjective conscious experience is not the same thing as its neurological substrate, I'm not quite ready to follow him all the way into unadulterated free-will. Neuroscientist and experimental psychologist

Stanislas Dehaene states the matter thus: "Our brain states are clearly not uncaused and do not escape the laws of physics. ... But our decisions are genuinely free whenever they are based on a conscious deliberation that proceeds autonomously without any impediment, weighing the pros and cons before committing to a course of action."[11]

Does our behavior—and the decision-making leading to our behavior—escape the iron law of nature that every effect has a cause? It seems to me that each human being is, as it were, a matrix, or node, in nature's chain of cause and effect. Simple behaviors often have simple causes: I inadvertently touch a hot pan, feel pain, and immediately move my hand away. (In this instance, a reflex arc is already in the process of moving my hand away by the time I become consciously aware of the pain.) But more complex behaviors—those involving difficult decision-making, choices that pit self-interest or pleasure against a sense of duty or morality, or other conflicting considerations, including conflicting pleasures, duties, or needs—will result from a vast array of inputs, many of which will operate on a more or less subconscious level. There will be sensory inputs, informing me of the current situation. There will be memories, recent and distant, pleasant and unpleasant, but in any case informative, that have a bearing on my decision. There will be, stored within the neural circuitry of my brain, the likes and dislikes and the values that I have acquired on life's journey and that contribute to my sense of self and of what makes me feel shame, pride, satisfaction, dissatisfaction—we are, after all, social creatures. Some of my inclinations and aversions are clearly influenced by genetics. More primordially, there are the instincts to survive and to reproduce—instincts without which we would not be here. Out of this vast array of inputs, many of which we are but dimly aware, comes a decision, and hence a behavior.[12]

Thus, one can retain a notion of individual responsibility and even of agency, even though that agency is not independent of the law of cause and effect. Clearly, society would be unworkable without the notion of individual accountability, and that realization is a part of the information stored in our mental circuitry. Our mental equipment includes an awareness of our responsibility for our actions. And the nodal quality of our agency is significant: many factors, any one of which or even any group of which might otherwise have no effect, come together (or reach a threshold) in the brain and produce an output, an act, a change upon the world.

This analysis of "free will" leads to this further mystery: If all of the aspects of our subjective consciousness, including our willful behavior, are the result of physiological, neural processes, then of what use is our experience of subjective consciousness? Is it possible that even our most complex, sophisticated, morally charged behaviors could occur without our conscious awareness? If so, why did conscious awareness evolve? What is its adaptive value? And if not—if our subjective awareness is somehow needed in order to do the things that we do, then *how can that be?* Science does not allow for the material world to be acted upon by something as nonmaterial as awareness or thought per se. If the underlying neural processes weigh all the inputs and determine our behavior, what then is the role of conscious awareness itself? Even Kant recognized this "antinomy," as did Leibniz before him. Is this a convincing argument for the belief, held by many writers in this field, that subjective conscious experience and its underlying neural processes must amount to the same thing?

Some theories have been advanced in recent years as to the adaptive value of subjective feelings. Computer scientist David Gelernter, in his *The Tides of Mind*, states the problem: "[I]f not being conscious would not impede our performance, why are we conscious?" His answer is that the experience of emotion is a more effective memory cue than mere computer-like—or zombie-like—cognition. "The *felt* emotion might conceivably

8

reach, discover, activate, summon more memories—reach farther and deeper—than the unfelt, merely thought-about emotion." Restating this point, Gelernter observes, "Without emotion as a cue to recollection, your memory would be a mere database, a mere computer."[13] Why does this matter? Because, says Gelernter, enhanced memory gives rise to enhanced creativity—a distinct advantage.

Similarly, neuroscientist Antonio Damasio finds that computer-like rationality and cognition is not enough for us to thrive; our behavior must be informed not only by reason but by feeling. He cites data showing that emotional flatness, resulting from frontal-lobe damage, seriously impairs decision-making ability.

British psychologist Nicholas Humphrey, in his book *Soul Dust*, suggests that the subjective experience of pleasure and pain—not only those of a purely physical nature but more sublime experiences as well—enhances our motivation to survive and thrive. He quotes from poets and artists of every genre to illustrate the powerfully motivating force of our emotional responses to simply being in the world, a world full of meaning for us, wherever we turn our gaze. This is particularly important for us humans because, by comparison to other species, our behaviors are relatively less influenced by instinct and more by thought and feeling. Additionally, Humphrey asserts that our introspective consciousness of selfhood leads us to an empathetic awareness of the conscious selfhood of others, which in turn strengthens social cooperation, which is adaptive in terms of species survival. Perhaps the most obvious adaptive advantage of the "social intelligence" aspect of consciousness is that, as Humphrey notes, it enabled our ancestors—and enables us—to predict (to an important extent) the behavior of others.

But as arresting and eloquently stated as Gelernter's, Damasio's, and Humphrey's theories are, the problem remains: either our thoughts and feelings *are* our underlying neural processes, or they are not; either answer is, as we've seen, problematic. Humphrey's position seems particularly puzzling: he's very clear that indeed our thoughts and feelings *are* those neural processes and nothing else, yet if that's so, then why do we need these life-enhancing subjective experiences?[14] And if, conversely, our subjective experience of thought and feeling is not reducible to the underlying neural processes, then how can these non-material experiences possibly affect the real world in any way? Is conscious experience a causal agent or a mere epiphenomenon—a useless by-product of neurophysiological processes that do the actual work of living our lives?

We have, I think, gotten a taste of the ineffable quality of subjective consciousness. Science cannot explain why I experience just this subjective consciousness, even as science seems to be increasingly able to explain the physiological, neural underpinnings of subjective consciousness. But as philosopher David Chalmers has observed, there appears to be a "Hard Problem," or explanatory gap: for every subjective experience, thought, feeling, perception, and act of will, there is a neurophysiological process that appears to be its cause. But how? How do we get from objective neural processes to subjective experiences? This question has been asked for centuries—Pascal observed that "Man... cannot conceive... how a material body can be united to a mind."[15] But with recent advances in neuroscience, a vast literature has appeared over the past several decades to debate the issue: is there an explanatory gap between objective neural processes and subjective experience, or not? Philosophers, psychologists, neurobiologists, linguists, computer scientists, and others have made their contributions to this controversy. Some of them—philosophers Thomas Nagel and Colin McGinn and neurologist Raymond Tallis—have agreed that there is indeed a Hard Problem, or explanatory gap. Even a famous contemporary novelist has weighed in. In Ian McEwan's novel *Saturday*, his neurosurgeon hero, committed as he is to reductive science, nonetheless reflects, while operating on a patient's brain, that after science gives us all of its answers, "the wonder will remain. That mere wet stuff can make this bright inward cinema of thought, of sight and sound and touch bound into a vivid illusion of... a self. ... Could it ever be explained, how matter becomes conscious?"[16]

Much research and theoretical work in recent years and decades points to recursive circuitry in the brain, intersecting with more primitive (from an evolutionary standpoint) stimulus-response circuitry as a requirement, or a correlate, of consciousness. Many specific parts of the brain have been identified as areas where the inputs from the various sense organs are processed, memories are stored and retrieved, language is produced and comprehended—and so forth and so on—and behavior is executed. But does all of this explain "how matter becomes conscious"?

In contrast to the writers mentioned above, many others—Daniel Dennett prominent among them—have asserted that if the underlying neurophysiological bases of subjective experience can be explained, the mystery disappears. Yet at the conclusion of his *Consciousness Explained*, Dennett concedes that his explanation of consciousness is "far from complete," and that it replaces one set of metaphors for another.[17] In fact—perhaps puzzlingly, given their physicalist orientation—Dennett and his colleague Douglas Hofstadter (*The Mind's I*, p. 8) state the matter well: "How can living physical bodies in the physical world produce such a phenomenon? Science has revealed the secrets of many initially mysterious natural phenomena—magnetism or photosynthesis or digestion are in principle equally accessible to any observer with the right apparatus, but any particular case of consciousness seems to have a favored or privileged observer. ... For this reason and others, so far there is no good theory of consciousness."[18]

But in defense of his physicalist thesis, Dennett appears to do an about-face: he points to other areas of science—

chemistry, physics, biology—wherein physical explanations of events are readily accepted, and asks why consciousness should be any different.[19] Similarly, John Searle (*Minds, Brains and Science*)[20] likens the relationship between consciousness and its neurophysiological underpinnings to the "macro" level of physical reality (accessible to the unaided senses) and the "micro"—molecular—level. The analogy fails. With suitable apparatus we can (at least in theory) observe things all the way down from the macro to the micro level, *including every level in between*. Neither Searle nor Dennett has shown us what lies between the objective processes of the brain and subjective conscious experience. To claim that there is nothing in between physical process and conscious experience defeats the analogy.

Searle and Dennett invite us to consider various biological processes. Let's consider vision. The physical processes that allow us to see colors like red or green involve measurable things like wavelengths as well as light- and color-sensitive nerve cells in the retina. But we normally *experience* none of these things; we experience something *unmeasurable*, such as the redness of red or the greenness of green. Dennett accuses us of mistakenly thinking that his explanation leaves something out. But as we've seen, it *does* leave something out. Objectively observable physical changes cause other objectively observable physical changes. But when my physiological apparatus causes me to feel pain, or love, or a sensation of red, I must ask: How did we get from objective, measurable physical processes to subjective, immeasurable experience—what philosophers of consciousness call "qualia"?[21] As the famous neurologist Oliver Sacks said, "Something beyond our understanding occurs in the genesis of qualia, the transformation of an objective cerebral computation to a subjective experience. Philosophers argue endlessly over how these transformations occur and whether we will ever be capable of understanding them."[22]

Other prominent writers, including Steven Pinker and Antonio Damasio, have admitted that science may not be able to explain the gap, though Damasio is optimistic. Neuroscientist Christof Koch goes so far as to assert that doubt concerning science's ability to eventually understand consciousness "is a particularly pernicious myth, because it inhibits research."[23] Can Koch, or anyone else, point to any research that has been "inhibited"? Koch lists some of the many advances in the understanding of the neurological correlates of consciousness, and proclaims, "These advances have not solved the hard problem, to be sure, but there is little reason for pessimism that they won't eventually." These amazing advances, and those to come, are certainly to be welcomed, as is all scientific knowledge, but none of them have brought us any closer to understanding how this wet stuff in my head causes this bright inward cinema—my subjective conscious experience.

Two distinguished scientists—Nobel laureate Gerald Edelman (*Wider Than the Sky*) and neuroscientist and psychologist Mark Solms (*The Hidden Spring*)—have attempted to address both the Hard Problem (or mind-body problem) and the adaptiveness-of-consciousness problem—that is to say, given the scientific and philosophical prohibition against non-material and non-objective things like feelings causing material, objective things to happen (e.g., nerve firings, behavior, etc.), how can subjective consciousness (including feelings) be adaptive? Why would we have evolved to have subjective consciousness if it can have no practical effect? Solms, throughout his book, appears to reject this scientific and philosophical prohibition, insisting instead that "feelings really *do* something—and they greatly increase our chances of survival in the process."[24] How can this be? Edelman says it *cannot* be: "According to the laws of physics, the causal order is closed—that is, it cannot be affected directly by mental properties such as qualia [including feelings]." And: "Consciousness is a property of neural processes and cannot in itself act causally in the world. ... [T]he neural bases of consciousness, not consciousness itself, can cause things to happen."[25]

Despite their opposite views on the causal efficacy of feelings, Edelman and Solms appear to be in somewhat closer—but not entire—agreement regarding the relationship between subjective consciousness and neural processes. Edelman insists that the neural processes associated (or correlated) with conscious experience *entail* that experience; this means (as quoted above) that subjective consciousness is a *property* of the corresponding neural processes. Similarly (perhaps), Solms says that consciousness and neural processes "are parallel manifestations of a single underlying process. ... Physiological and psychological phenomena can... be reduced to unitary causes, but not to each other."[26] But the mystery remains: How does it come about that subjective consciousness is a property, a parallel manifestation, or—as other writers say—an effect of neural processes?

It seems to me that Edelman and others attempt to reduce the explanatory gap by trying to explain away subjective consciousness. In Edelman's view, qualia (the feeling of pain, the experience of blue, red, etc.) are simply "discriminations." "['H]eat' is not 'green,' 'green' is not 'touch,' etc."[27] A former student of Edelman's, Anil Seth (*Being You*) similarly proposes: "[T]he 'what-it-is-like-ness' of any specific conscious experience is defined not by what it *is*, but by all the unrealized but possible things that it is *not*. An experience of pure redness is the way that it is, not because of any intrinsic property of 'redness' but because red is not blue, green, or any other color... or indeed any other mental content whatsoever."[28]

But "what-it-is-like-ness" is the whole point—the defining characteristic of subjective consciousness—and it is not furnished by "discriminations" and "is-nots." We experience red not merely as not green (etc.) but as *red*. And the emotions

14

that we often experience in association with colors (etc.) can hardly be accounted for by the mere fact that one color (or whatever) is not another.

Anil Seth goes on to set forth neuroscientist Giulio Tononi's Integrated Information Theory (IIT), yet another attempt to reduce subjective conscious experience to its physiological substrates and to ignore the *qualitative*, as opposed to *quantitative*, aspects of experience.

Neuroscientist Michael Graziano of Princeton presents a theory that, at first blush, struck me as intriguing. His Attention Schema Theory goes something like this: Various neural circuits continually focus attention by reinforcing certain external and internal inputs and demoting others. Additional circuitry produces a schema of this attention process, which, in turn, produces "awareness." "Awareness is a description of attention." Graziano repeats this theme in many iterations: "The schema provides a depiction of what it means for a brain to deeply process, apprehend, attend to, and *seize* [Graziano's emphasis] information." And: "Awareness itself... is a complex, continuously recomputed model that describes what it means— the conditions, dynamics, and consequences—for a brain to attentively process information."[29] The underlying notion is that my brain, through this attention-schema process, convinces me that I'm having conscious experience, that I am a self, and that other people are also conscious, experiencing selves.

An obvious question leaps out: Where, or who, is this "I" that is being "convinced" that it is an I? Who (what part of my brain) is "aware"? The mystery of internal subjective experience remains, as Graziano himself seems forced to admit: "When information is processed in the brain in some... as yet undetermined way, a subject's experience of awareness emerges. ... [F]or unknown reasons, you have a conscious experience of greenness."[30]

But that's the whole point, isn't it? No exposition of neural circuitry, no Attention Schema Theory, no Multiple Drafts

Model (Dennett), no "strange loops" (Douglas Hofstadter), no Integrated Information Theory (Tononi, Seth), no microtubules (Roger Penrose[31]), not even a "global neuronal workspace" (Bernard Baars, Dehaene), however compelling (or not) these theories may be, can explain my experience, not of wavelengths or differentials but of the color green, when I look out at my lawn on a spring or summer day. And as Graziano himself says (above), "*You* [my emphasis] have a conscious experience of greenness." He doesn't say, "there is a consciousness of greenness."

The weakness of Graziano's "consciousness is information" mantra becomes increasingly evident in the later chapters. He proposes that computers might someday have humanlike "awareness," and/or that people will perhaps be able to download their consciousness to a computer and thus escape the grim reaper. He suggests another path to (partial—or "low-resolution") immortality: He was very close to his grandmother, and now that she's deceased, some of her thoughts and personality live on in him. Well and good. But the obvious fact is that his grandmother is no longer living and thus no longer *experiencing*. She is no longer conscious; she is, at this point, neither attending nor awaring (so to speak).

Like Graziano, but with much more detail, Solms lays out his case for the possibility that machines can be fashioned that will have subjective experience, including feelings. "[A]ny two systems with the same fine-grained functional organisation will have qualitatively identical experiences."[32] German philosopher Thomas Metzinger[33] is already laying out an ethics of subjectively conscious machines.

But a computer, no matter how powerful, does not owe its origin to biological processes or its continued existence to what are—or may be—the adaptive elements of subjective consciousness. Computers do not have interests of their own—what Heidegger called *Sorge*—in other words, computers don't care. Solms suggests that computers can be engineered to have survival needs, and will, therefore, "care" and "feel." The nerves and neurological structures involved in caring and feeling can, Solms suggests, be replicated by computer chips (or whatever). In other words, artificial needs and artificial feelings. I would be more convinced if we knew how it is that nerves and neurological structures produce feelings. But (*pace* Solms and all the many others), we don't. We do know this: We are products of biology, not of human technology, and we live in a world, and our continued existence depends upon our interaction with that world. As living organisms, we are vitally, intrinsically *interested*. Computers and robots are not.

At the outset of writing this book, I had assumed that my arguments would be largely directed against physicalism in its various guises, as described above. I did not anticipate the resurgence of such notions as panpsychism and idealism. Panpsychism posits that everything—not only animals but plants, rocks, and even electrons and other particles—have at least some level of conscious experience. However implausible and counterintuitive this notion may be, it has a long history, having been given credence by some of the most distinguished philosophers throughout the ages, and it seems to have found new life in the thought of some of today's thinkers. Both David Chalmers (philosopher) and Roger Penrose (physicist and mathematician) have suggested its possibility, and now a young British philosopher, Philip Goff,[34] has embraced panpsychism as the most likely key to solving the "Hard Problem," the puzzle as to how our subjective, qualitative experience arises from the grey matter of our brains. Building on the thought of Chalmers and others, Goff sees consciousness as a fundamental characteristic of the material universe, thus bridging the "mind-body" dichotomy. But if this theory were true, why is it that wherever we find convincing evidence of conscious experience (including in ourselves), that experience appears to be inseparable from not just any kinds of things but from neurons and from their connections and processes?

Philosophical idealism has been given new life by scientist and philosopher Bernardo Kastrup[35] and others. According to this view, there is a universal consciousness that is the sole primary aspect ("ontological primitive") of the universe; individual humans (and other conscious beings) are "dissociated alters" of the universal consciousness. The idea here is that all that we directly know is consciousness; the physical world is secondary, in that we know it only through conscious perception, and its existence consists in "excitations" of universal consciousness, or "mind-at-large." Ignored is the fact that every conscious "myself" lives in a world of "not-myself," and my selfhood arises only in relation to, and recognition of, the non-self. As the phenomenologists have taught us, all consciousness is, in one way or another, *consciousness of something*. And again, as Heidegger pointed out, consciousness as we know it involves *Sorge* — we care. I'm not clear as to the *Sorge* of "mind-at-large." As for the mysteries of consciousness that I have described above, they remain, for me, unresolved. As we've seen, the physicalists claim that consciousness is merely a "property" or "parallel manifestation" of brain activity; conversely, the idealists claim that brain activity is an "excitation" of consciousness. The explanatory gap remains, as does the primal mystery we started out with: Why am I me?

We are often told by reductionists that the mysteries of consciousness and selfhood are illusory. We've all seen examples of optical illusions — indeed, reductionist writers on consciousness are fond of using such examples to illustrate their point: lines that are, objectively, of the same length but appear to have different lengths because of other elements in the figure, or areas of grey that are, objectively, of the same intensity (value), but which appear to differ — again, because of surrounding elements. These are, in fact, illusions: we make judgments as to objective reality (influenced here by our figure/ground perception), and in these instances our judgments are erroneous. Similarly, delusions, such as those experienced in psychosis, are erroneous judgments as to objective facts. But the fact that I (not you or anyone else) am experiencing this self (not yours or anyone else's) is a *subjective* fact, not a matter of potentially conflicting judgments, as with objective facts. As neurologist Sam Harris says in his "The Mystery of Consciousness" podcast, "to say that consciousness may only *seem* to exist is to admit its existence in full—for if things seem any at all, *that* is consciousness."[36] Harris's wife, Annaka Harris, points out that if subjective conscious experience did not exist, how would we even be able to talk about it?[37]

. But oddly, the Harrises, along with Bruce Hood[38] (as well as Susan Blackmore and others, to be discussed in a later chapter), assert that the self is an illusion. Various arguments are presented. The self can be made to dissolve through meditation or drugs; it can wither away in dementia; our memories, by which the narrative self is constructed, are unreliable; we can, under social pressure or influence, behave in ways that are inconsistent with our values; there is no "Cartesian theater"—a specific place in the brain that is the seat of the self. Above all, "free will"—our sense of undetermined agency—is not, in fact, strictly undetermined. But do any or all of these arguments justify the conclusion that the self is an illusion?

Ironically, what Sam Harris said of consciousness can just as well be said of the self: To say that it only *seems* to exist is to admit its existence in full. The fact that the self is dependent upon the functioning of the brain does not explain it away, any more than that fact explains consciousness away. The fact that my sense of free will has an illusional aspect does not make my self illusional. "Free will" can be looked at from both an objective and a subjective standpoint, but "self"—i.e., *this* person, not that person or any other person—is pure subjectivity. As for memory, its distortion with the passage of time involves objective error, but not the subjective fact that my memories, accurate or not, are mine alone.[39]

What is the self? It is the individual, embodied, interested, subjective consciousness, and a sense of identity with, or ownership of, that consciousness. My subjective consciousness is "interested" in that it is not indifferent, and it is not indifferent precisely because (unlike computers) it is *embodied* in mortal flesh and blood, evolved over countless millennia, and is engaged in a world. I have desires, pains, likes and dislikes, and, importantly, memories—a private narrative. However ephemeral or distorted these memories may be, they are mine. Whatever else might be included in a concept of self, this embodied, interested, subjective consciousness is at its core.

All knowledge, however "objective" it may be, starts with individual subjectivity; if we can test our subjective perceptions and judgments against those of others, and against other evidence, we may arrive at a semblance of objective truth. But we cannot directly experience each other's subjectivity in the manner that we directly experience our own. Thus, my experience of myself as an unexplainable fact—a noumenon— is a purely subjective fact, untestable by outside observation. Objectivity is not, and cannot be, an issue here; hence, there can be no issue of illusion or delusion. Solms claims that "Strictly speaking, there is no essence that stays the same across time."[40] But if you're as old as I am, you can remember as far back as the 1940s. I was "me" then and I'm still "me" now, however much I may have changed in various respects and however accurate or inaccurate my memories may be.

As the writer and philosopher Jacques Maritain observed, "Subjectivity marks the frontier which separates the world of philosophy from the world of religion. ... Philosophy runs against an insurmountable barrier in attempting to deal with subjectivity, because while of course it knows subjects, it knows them only as objects."[41] Maritain was a Catholic, whereas I am a nonbeliever—a "nontheist," if you will. For me, religion has no power, in our modern world, to describe or explain objective reality; for that, we must turn to science. But as we've seen, science and philosophy have their limit, and Maritain has correctly identified that limit. Religion cannot give us explanations, but through the power of myth and metaphor it speaks to us of our humanity; it helps us to understand who we are. But before we look at religion and myth and art, we must look at the issue of meaning, which arises with the advent of human subjective consciousness as it transcends the world of instinct.

Chapter 2

Meaning

[F]or Modern Humans, analogy and metaphor pervade every aspect of our thought and lie at the heart of art, religion, and science.
Thomas Kuhn, "Metaphor in Science"

The famous mythographer Joseph Campbell once asserted that what folks are really looking for is not the meaning of life but the experience of living. In a sense, he was right: If we are to choose between a life of navel-gazing search for meaning and a life of adventure, accomplishment, and engagement, most of us would choose the latter. But choosing the latter will not make issues of meaning and meaningfulness go away. The existential psychotherapist Viktor Frankl, author of *Man's Search for Meaning*, wrote and spoke movingly of the role of meaning in his survival of Nazi death camps, an experience which, in turn, led him to the conviction that a successful search for—and acceptance of—meaning is essential to human well-being and to the therapeutic process. For Frankl, the search for meaning is not a retreat to navel-gazing but a call to action, to individual agency. Each individual's meaning is to be found not in one's self but in the world, the world in which one finds oneself, and he chided Abraham Maslow, a therapist famous and popular for his notion of "self-actualization." He chided his fellow existentialists also, for while they recognized that the individual is always in the world, they were reluctant to recognize that *meaning* is also in the world, and not an internal creation of the individual.

Before attempting to discern whether Campbell, Frankl, or the existentialists (or none of the above) are right, we should first look at the meaning of *meaning*—a word that, as anthropologist

Claude Lévy-Strauss said, is perhaps the most difficult word to define. Andrew Newberg et al., in *Why God Won't Go Away*,[1] provide an illustration: Picture an antelope and a prehistoric human in their respective habitats. In the bush or forest, a twig is heard to snap. Both the antelope and the human instantly experience a rush of adrenaline. They both stop and look toward the source of the sound. They see nothing. They wait. The antelope does nothing more than wait. Nothing happens— no lion or leopard appears—and eventually the antelope's adrenaline level subsides. The antelope moves on.

But the human does more than wait. The human wants to figure out what's going on. What caused the twig to snap? A dangerous beast? Or perhaps a smaller animal that could be killed for dinner? The human seeks the *meaning* of the sound.

How long is the road from the meaning of a sound in the forest to the meaning of life, of the universe, and of one's place therein? Whether long or not long, that early human was on the road.

This illustration tells us something essential about *meaning*: Meaning involves both emotion (e.g., fear, desire) and intellect, or cognition (reasoning, investigating). Newberg and colleagues observe that the human brain has evolved structures and connections that bring both emotion and cognition into play as we seek to make sense of our surroundings. "We need to extract meaning and relevance from the constant flood of sensory information bombarding our brains. ..."[2] Much like Kant (who lacked their neuroscientific knowledge), Newberg et al. posit certain innate "cognitive operators" (cf. Kant's categories) by means of which we make sense of our world. One of these operators is the "binary operator." "What could be more obvious than the notion that the opposite of 'up' is 'down'? But the relationship between 'up' and 'down' is not as absolute as it seems. In fact, it's really quite relative and arbitrary, and only feels obvious to us because our minds have evolved to see things that way."[3]

British archaeologist Steven Mithen applies the methods and insights of his discipline to the study of the evolution of human consciousness. Drawing on the work of Jerry Fodor and many other writers from a variety of disciplines, Mithen presents a modular concept of this evolution. Many animal species have a limited general intelligence; they have some capacity for learning, but much of their behavior is guided largely by instinct.[4] Chimpanzees, our closest relatives, have this type of intelligence, but also something else: a cognitive module, or specialized intelligence, geared specifically toward social relations. Unlike other animals, but like humans, chimpanzees know, when they look in a mirror, that they are seeing themselves. In dealing with other chimpanzees, they know how to practice deception; thus, they know that what they know (as individuals) and what other individuals know may not be the same thing. They have what psychologists call "theory of mind." We've seen, with Nicholas Humphrey (*supra*), the adaptive advantages of this social intelligence.

This was, essentially, the state of consciousness at the fork in the road, some six million years ago. But then our earliest hominid forebears began to branch off. In addition to the social module, they evolved other cognitive modules, notably, a toolmaking module and a module for assessing one's surroundings from the standpoint of important animals (game, or predators), plants, water supply, etc. Of course chimpanzees and even other animals, including birds, fashion and use rudimentary tools for specific tasks, but as early hominid species developed a specialized toolmaking intelligence, concerted effort and skill was devoted to the fabrication of multipurpose stone and wood tools.

Mithen notes that the Neanderthals, one of the very last of our non-*sapiens* forebears, were highly skilled at toolmaking, though with a very limited repertoire and with very little development over many thousands of years. They had social skills, they cared for their sick and injured, and they probably communicated vocally, though without grammar and without the limitless possibilities of expression afforded by full-fledged language. But here's the thing: They appear to have had no art and no religion. They did not decorate their bodies or adorn the tombs of their dead. They had no culture, as we normally think of it. Why?

Mithen explains that for the Neanderthals, the walls between their cognitive modules were too impenetrable. Without what Mithen calls cognitive fluidity—the breaking down of those walls—the cognitive connections that allow for analogy and metaphor (see the Kuhn epigraph at the beginning of this chapter) could not have occurred, and thus, no culture as we know it.

But as the days of the Neanderthals were waning, our species, *homo sapiens*, was coming to the fore. Early on, cracks were appearing in the walls, and those individuals who could make connections between the various modules (social, toolmaking, environmental) had a competitive advantage. Ultimately, cognitive fluidity came to predominate, and as the walls fell away, connections were made; analogy, symbols (including true language), and metaphor emerged; and art burst forth as if from the forehead of Zeus,[5] along with religious ideas and culture. One might say that *meaning* took on a whole new meaning.

This should not lead us to conclude, as many thinkers do (see next chapter) that art and religion sprang directly from the process of evolution. Cognitive fluidity made analogy possible— indeed, inevitable. Concurrently, the ability to conceptualize— to imagine—beyond the boundaries of immediate perception began to develop more fully. The human imagination began to soar toward the transcendent—the imperceptible.

In his book *Michelangelo's Finger*, British neurologist Raymond Tallis helps us to understand *meaning* and *duality* (binary thinking) and the development of what we might call transcendent consciousness—the human characteristic of being aware of much more than meets the eye (and other sense organs). Tallis approaches the issue of transcendent consciousness from an interesting and illustrative angle: *pointing*. Have you ever noticed that nonhuman animals totally don't get the concept of pointing? If you point to where the stick is, your dog has no idea what you're doing. The smartest of apes are no better at this. But from an early age, human children understand pointing; they understand what's happening when someone points, and they are able (and eager) to point themselves. When a parent (or other person) points, the child looks in the direction of the pointing to see what's there. For animals, by contrast, there's no *there* there. *There* is an abstraction, and animals don't do abstraction. Until we look toward what is being pointed to (and this requires at least a redirection of our attention and possibly of our spatial position), there is no *thing* but rather an abstract *possibility* or a *concept*, inaccessible to our furry friends. Pointing has *meaning*; it signifies "look there; there's something there that I see but you don't see and may want to see." Meaning transcends the merely given, the raw inputs of our sense organs.

To understand pointing is to understand two things: "the otherness of the world and the presence of other minds."[6] Tallis elaborates: "A world is a boundless sphere of shared possibility."[7] Thus we find ourselves in a world that we share with other conscious humans and at the same time we are confronted with separateness: I am in the world, as are you—we're in this together—but I am not the world and I am not you.

This shared world of possibility, beyond the sensibly given, "[t]he invisible, the insensible, the yonder, draws us onward" ultimately to "the beyond beyond all beyondering"[8]—a beyondness inaccessible to the organs of sense and the instruments of science, a beyondness accessible only to abstract imagination, including the religious imagination—a realm that even atheists, such as Tallis and I, can appreciate.

Another scientist, Edward O. Wilson, firmly planted in the soil of materialist reductionism, similarly observes: "Our minds travel easily—eagerly!—from the familiar and tangible to the mystic realm."[9]

In perhaps his most widely read book, *Civilization and Its Discontents*, Freud begins by quoting a friend, who chided Freud because he "failed to appreciate the real source of religiosity. This was a particular feeling of which he himself was never free, which he had found confirmed by others... a feeling that he was inclined to call a sense of 'eternity,' a feeling of something limitless, unbounded—as it were, 'oceanic.' This feeling was a purely subjective fact, not an article of faith; ... On the basis of this oceanic feeling alone one was entitled to call oneself religious, even if one rejected every belief and every illusion."[10] Freud himself experienced no such feelings, but I suspect that he was much more the exception than the rule. Even if we don't dwell in oceanic feeling from day to day, I suspect that most of us harbor a sense of the boundless beyond which calls to us—even those of us who believe in no god. When we look out across the sea, or up to the starry heavens, we experience that numinous, oceanic feeling.

We can begin to understand that art and religion would have begun to develop when human consciousness made the leap from the immanent to the transcendent—the vertical cognition described by Tallis as well as the horizontal cognition described by Mithen. But art and religion are not instincts; they arise from the vertical and horizontal cognition that evolved in the human species. Other species live largely by instinct. Their world is closely circumscribed and immanent, devoid of Rudolf Otto's ineffable "wholly other" (see next chapter) and of Pascal's "infinite immensity of spaces." There is no room—and no need—for art, religion, science, or philosophy in that world. But we humans, "bereft of instinct," as anthropologist Loren Eiseley said, "must search constantly for meanings."[11]

Psychologist Erich Fromm pointed out that the waning of instinct, and the waxing of human cognition beyond the immediately given, introduced an experience of separateness. "What is essential in the existence of man is the fact that he has emerged from the animal kingdom, from instinctive adaptation, that he has transcended nature. ... [O]nce thrown out of paradise—an original oneness with nature—cherubim with flaming swords block his way, if he should try to return." Fromm continues: "When man is born, the human race as well as the individual, he is thrown out of a situation which was definite, as definite as the instincts, into a situation which is indefinite, uncertain, and open."[12] Fromm goes on to speak of life being aware of itself, and of our experience of separateness, and our lifelong struggle to overcome separateness and to find some sort of unity with others.

Robinson Jeffers, whose poems evoke the beautiful, sublime, and at times frightening (storms, lightning, forest fires) aspects of the central California coast, was not only an early environmentalist but was also deeply interested in human consciousness. Like Fromm, Jeffers saw human consciousness, metaphorically, as The Fall. According to George Hart, "Jeffers considered consciousness as a sort of original sin, the blot on the race that divorces it from nature. ... Consciousness is the Fortunate Fall in evolution—without it we would not know that we are a part of the universe, but with it we are apart from the universe."[13]

And Loren Eiseley again: "Man fell from the grace of instinct into a confused and troubled cultural realm beyond nature. ..."[14]

This separateness from nature—even though we are, biologically, a part of nature—not only impels us toward breaking down our separateness from our fellow humans. As Raymond Tallis has eloquently explained, our evolved awareness, which transcends the immediately given, impels us toward that which is beyond the immediately given and ultimately toward the infinite or transcendent.

Fromm addresses this important point as well: "This need for transcendence is one of the most basic needs of man, rooted in the fact of his self-awareness, in the fact that he is not satisfied with the role of the creature, that he cannot accept himself as dice thrown out of the cup."[15] Fromm recognizes here that the mystery of selfhood (why am I me) and the human quest for transcendence are vitally linked.

We can see now that Viktor Frankl was only partly right. We cannot create meaning in ourselves. But neither is meaning "out there." Meaning can only arise in our encounter with the world. And thus Joseph Campbell was only partly right as well. As philosopher Martin Buber (*I and Thou*) famously said, "All real living is meeting."[16] And as we've seen, meaning and meeting are inseparable.

Much the same idea was articulated by French philosopher Maurice Merleau-Ponty, one of the leading phenomenologists and existentialists of the mid-twentieth century. As explained by Eric Matthews, Merleau-Ponty saw that the world is not an abstraction; rather, "it is the place in which we live, ... so that the meanings of things, in a sense, exist neither 'inside' our minds nor in the world itself, but in the space between us and the world."[17]

With the evolution of human consciousness, we see the emergence and compelling importance of the dualities of human experience: subject and object, self and world, self and other, the immanent and the transcendent, the past and the future, the sacred and the profane, clean and unclean, the Apollonian (rational) and the Dionysian (nonrational), conscious and subconscious, yin and yang, animus (male) and anima (female), good and evil, life and death. Other animals don't think about these dualities. They don't think about transcendence. They just try—instinctively—to survive. But we humans are in Hamlet's soliloquy. We sail, with Odysseus, upon the wine-dark sea.

The structural anthropologist Claude Lévy-Strauss observed that all myths are attempts at dealing with these dualities. As we've seen, not the least of our dualities is that of self and non-self—other selves, nature, and the beyond. With the emergence of human consciousness comes the emergence of meaning and of duality. Art, myth, metaphor, symbols, and religion must inevitably follow.

Chapter 3

Beauty and the Arts

On a visit to the Grand Canyon, I reflected upon the fact that the wondrous beauty of the Grand Canyon is not an attribute of the Grand Canyon itself, which is, after all, merely a vast, meaningless hole in the ground, nor is its wondrous beauty merely my creation, or even the creation of humankind in general. How, then, are we to explain the wondrous beauty of the Grand Canyon?[1]

Some rather prosaic, utilitarian, instinct-based explanations have been advanced for our preferences for certain kinds of landscapes, etc. (see Denis Dutton's *The Art Instinct*, for example—although it's difficult to see how the uninhabitable Grand Canyon would fit Dutton's utilitarian theory). I believe that we will not find the answer in such theories. We've seen in the previous chapter that as *homo sapiens* developed, instinctual behavior waned and was largely replaced by the interplay of emotion and cognition to form meaning and to guide behavior. And as we saw, meaning arises not purely "in here" nor "out there" but in *encounter* (or, as Buber preferred to say, *meeting*). The Grand Canyon is a vast, rocky hole in the ground. Our brains are a vast bundle of nerve cells. But in the *encounter* between the subjectivity created by those nerve cells and the Other—the non-self out there—a new reality, a new *meaning*, is created.

How so? Why do feelings of beauty and awe emerge from our encounter with the Grand Canyon, or with the ocean, or with the starry heavens? Many theories, some of them supported by modern neuroscience, have been put forth to explain various aspects of our appreciation for nature, art, music, and so forth. But is there, or will there ever be, a complete explanation? I think not. Nevertheless, I believe that both the appreciation of beauty and of the arts as well as the ubiquity of religion have, in addition to neurological aspects which will be touched on below, an aspect of the numinous, a concept based on what Rudolf Otto, in *The Idea of the Holy*, calls the *numen*. Not unlike Kant's *noumenon*—that which is uncaused; that which can be an object of thought but not of perception—Otto's *numen* (a word of Latin origin, not Greek) is not subject to rational description. Objectively, a *numen* (that which is numinous, to put it another way) can be nothing more than, say, a vast hole in the ground, yet in our encounter with it we find ourselves "quite beyond the sphere of the usual, the intelligible, and the familiar"[2] and in the presence of the *mysterium tremendum*, the "wholly other." "Sublime" and "ineffable" are other words that Otto uses, and at one point he uses the word "grace"; thus we are reminded that the numinous encounter is nonrational and "full of grace," even for those of us who (unlike Otto, who was a devout Lutheran Christian) reject supernaturalism. In the presence of the numinous, we feel both humbled and exalted.

The encounter with the numinous—that which inspires feelings of numinosity—is the precursor to religion and also to art. Rudolf Otto addresses the expression of the numinous in art and architecture and music. In this connection, Otto is particularly interested in negatives: darkness, silence, void. "The semi-darkness that glimmers in vaulted halls, or beneath the branches of a lofty forest glade, strangely quickened by the mysterious play of half-lights, has always spoken eloquently to the soul, and the builders of temples, mosques, and churches have made full use of it."[3] I see something of this aspect in the landscapes of Corot, and in Sargent's *Street in Venice*. I have long been struck, also, by the use of grey by Matisse, a painter known for his bright colors. More recently, abstract artists have provided powerful examples. The areas of blank canvas— partially covered, to varying degrees, by bands or patches of color (or black)—in the works of Morris Louis, Clyfford Still,[4] and Franz Kline recall for me Rudolf Otto's theory of the numinous void: "For 'void' is, like darkness and silence, a negation, but a negation that does away with every 'this' and 'here' in order that the 'wholly other' may become actual."[5]

The inadequacy of reductionist, instinct-based theories regarding the origin and function of art is illustrated—unintentionally—by the aforementioned Denis Dutton. In *The Art Instinct*, Dutton presents his "Darwinian aesthetics," wherein the purpose of "the arts in all their glory" is to "amuse, shock, titillate, and enrapture."[6] On the next page, he introduces one of his "Darwinian" concepts: landscape painting depicts landscape features that are salubrious for human life. Later in the book, Dutton presents another utilitarian concept: the art of fiction in all of its forms arose from storytelling, which, for our primeval ancestors, had these adaptive features: (1) exploring alternate strategies for responding to threats or opportunities; (2) transmitting useful information; and (3) "exploring the points of view, beliefs, motivations, and values of other human minds."[7]

As to the overarching question—What is art?—Dutton provides a long list of criteria, including "pleasure," "virtuosity," "novelty," and the amount of "shop talk" generated by the artwork.[8]

Daniel Levitin, an expert on music and on the neurological and psychological aspects thereof, has written an interesting and informative book, *This Is Your Brain on Music*. He confirms insights relating to emotion and cognition that we encountered in Newberg et al. (previous chapter) and that we'll encounter presently in Kandel, Lehrer, and Calvin. He acknowledges the ultimately ineffable quality of our emotional response to music—who among us has never marveled at how a purely physical object like a guitar, a piano, a violin, or a horn can be caused to produce sounds that profoundly move us emotionally?

But in his last chapter he makes what is, to me, a somewhat jarring assertion: Music is an instinct. If this is so, then it must be that those of our ancestors who had music were better able to survive and reproduce than those who lacked music. Like Dutton, Levitin quotes Darwin on the role of music in sexual selection[9] (like birds, humans use music to woo prospective mates), and on music as a precursor to language.

British science writer Philip Ball has a book called *The Music Instinct*. The title of this very interesting and informative book is misleading. Although Ball joins Levitin—and Darwin—in extolling music's aphrodisiacal powers, he lays out the case for why music is probably *not* an instinct. "Are there... any brain regions that are dedicated *specifically* to musical tasks? ... If there are, it would suggest that music is innate, engineered by evolution—which in turn would imply that it serves an adaptive function, that musicality somehow helped our ancestors to be productively successful. ... [T]hat quest [for specialized music modules in the brain] has so far failed to produce definite results."[10] In fact, "[W]hereas many cognitive tasks, such as vision or language, have fairly well-localized centres of brain activation, music does not. ... [W]hen we listen to music, all the lights are apt to come on at once. Pretty much the whole brain may become active: motor centres that govern movement, the 'primal' emotion centres, the language modules that serve to process syntax and semantics, the auditory highways. ... [I]t is a whole-brain phenomenon."[11]

Ball quotes neuroscientist Aniruddh Patel: "The notion that something is either a product of biological adaptation or a frill (Steven Pinker) is based on a false dichotomy. Music may be a human invention, but if so, it resembles the ability to make and control fire: it is something we invented that transforms human life."[12]

I believe that the weight of evidence suggests that music (and the arts generally) are not so much an instinct as an outgrowth of the expanded powers of human consciousness which take us beyond the immediately given, beyond biological needs, and impels our search for meaning and transcendence. For birds, "music" is indeed an instinct. Their repertoire is limited, as are the uses to which their "music" is applied—warning of danger, attracting mates. And pure enjoyment does not appear to be one of those uses. Despite Levitin's efforts, neither he nor Dutton—nor even the great Darwin himself—makes a convincing case that human music was ever so essential to mating, or any other life-sustaining, species-sustaining function, as to be evolutionarily adaptive. Human music is generative (unlimited in its repertoire, even within parameters) in much the same way as human language.[13] Music is a source of enjoyment and emotional enrichment for its own sake, and the emotions that it arouses tend not to be those associated with immediate preservation of life, such as fear or anger.

Humans may well be endowed with the neurological equipment for both music and language—as we've seen, humans are equipped to seek and find meaning in their encounter with the world, and this equipment, more than instinct, strikes me as the stage-setting for music and the arts, as well as religion. As Ball says: "Perhaps one of the keys to music's power is that we are beings that have evolved to try to interpret information and to project meaning on to it. ... It is precisely because the meaning eludes us—because, indeed, there is none we can articulate—that we come back to it again and again."[14] And quoting the composer Aaron Copland: "[Music] may express a state of meaning for which there exists no adequate word in any language."[15]

In rejecting reductionist notions such as Dutton's "art instinct" and Levitin's "music instinct," we need not reject neuroscientific explanations, as far as they can take us. Nobel laureate Eric Kandel[16] makes some interesting and pertinent observations (including the neurophysiological underpinnings) of the human brain's responses to art. When we look at representational art—

even if it's impressionistic or surrealistic—we recognize the inhabitants (objects and people) of our world. This is consistent with our adaptively evolved capabilities of perception and cognition. But when we look at abstract artworks, the usual frames of reference are missing; instead we see not objects but abstractions: color, line, etc. divorced from recognizable objects. We are in a quandary: we need to try to make sense of this. But if we are to engage with the work, we must allow free rein to emotion, both conscious and subconscious. If there is meaning to be had, it will not be handed to us on a platter but will emerge from a creative encounter—a relational event.

Both representational and nonrepresentational artworks invite us to engage with human sensibility, emotion, and creativity. Even such seemingly emotionless works as those of Piet Mondrian are an assertion of human understanding over against the raw stuff of nature, of essence over raw existence.

Jonah Lehrer (*Proust Was a Neuroscientist*) is a former research colleague of Kandel's. Studying the works of great artists in various genres, as well as the artists' commentary on their own work, Lehrer shows how the intent and achievement of these artists prefigured the findings of neuroscience. Although problems have been alleged with regard to some of Lehrer's other works, there are interesting and valid observations in this book. As with the paintings of Cézanne, so also with the music of Stravinsky: Great art challenges the mind to fill in the blanks, to imagine that which is absent, to give form to that which seems formless, to make sense where sense is not evident, to find meaning in a world in which only humans can do so.

Similarly, William H. Calvin, in *A Brief History of the Mind*, observes: "*Discovering hidden patterns* [Calvin's emphasis] is seen in music, jigsaw puzzles, and doing science. We take great pleasure in 'getting it.' We love to see patterns emerging from seeming chaos... Coherence-finding is probably part of the source of our musical pleasure..."[17]

Unsurprisingly, Oliver Sacks has some interesting things to say about music and human consciousness. "Keeping time, physically and mentally, depends... on interactions between the auditory and the dorsal premotor cortex—and it is only in the human brain that a functional connection between these two areas exists. Crucially, these sensory and motor activations are precisely integrated with each other."[18] And, quoting from Victor Zuckerkandl (Sound and Symbol): "Hearing a melody is hearing, having heard, and being about to hear all at once. Every melody declares to us that the past can be there without being remembered, the future without being foreknown."[19]

But as useful and stimulating—and no doubt true—as these contributions are, there is, I believe, more to be said about the emergence of art, and of religion (not that they're the same) in our species. Raymond Tallis[20] lays this out with his customary insightfulness. Unlike the world of other species, our human world transcends the immediately given objects of our senses. Thus, we inhabit not merely an immediate environment but a world of both the given and the possible, the immanent and the transcendent. Only in such a world—a world inhabited by humans—can there be questions of truth and untruth; only here can be found ethics and aesthetics, art and religion.

In addition, Tallis explains that "a fundamental impulse of the artist (and the delight afforded by art) is rooted in the need to satisfy, if only intermittently, the hunger to be entirely where one is, so that subjective reality and objective situation coincide, and experiences are fully experienced."[21] Purely descriptive language, no matter how eloquent, can never be adequate to the fullness and particularity of experience.

Surely we have all experienced wonderful moments that were interrupted by the sad thought that this wonderful moment will soon pass, and no photograph or recording, nor even memory itself, could possibly allow us to relive it in all of its original glory and power. "Abide, moment!" as Nietzsche said. This is part of the noble tragedy of human life. But there's this partial consolation: our wonderful moments are enriched by conscious and/or subconscious memories of previous experiences, and our future moments will be enriched by the memory, however diminished from its original splendor, of this moment.

The arts, from their first beginnings, have been our means of conquering raw facticity, the cold, indifferent empire of existence. The creative, artistic act is the triumph of human *being* over contingent *existence*. We will explore this central theme further in the next chapter with the help of Sartre's short novel *Nausea*.

Throughout much of my life a central avocation of mine has been portrait drawing and painting. I sensed, early on, that I find myself in an "I-Thou" relation with the model/subject, regardless of the latter's gender, age, race/ethnicity, or degree of physical attractiveness. Empathy is, of course, an element of this relation, but it cannot be the whole story. Paradoxically, the model/subject is a fellow human with whom I empathize but also *wholly other* and inaccessible. French philosopher Emmanuel Levinas recognized that the face of the Other is at once infinitely vulnerable and infinitely transcendent: the face reveals the Other as object, for all the world to look at and judge and compare, yet the face also reveals the "infinite Other," transcending all description, measure, and judgment.

Buber (*I and Thou*), in describing the process of creating art, said, "In bodying forth, I disclose."[22] The numinosity of subjective feeling is brought into the objective world, and if that creation is artistically successful it can disclose, to the receptive eye, new possibilities, new appreciations, new numinosities. As art critic Sir Herbert Read put it: "[Art] gives concrete existence to what is numinous, what is beyond the limits of rational discourse: it brings the dynamics of subjective experience to a point of rest in the concrete object."[23]

As we'll see in the next chapter, art and religion are not one and the same, but they both arise inevitably, not from instinct but from the nature of human consciousness. As such, every aesthetic or artistic feeling or act, and every religious feeling or act, has its neurological correlate. But just as science cannot resolve the mysteries of subjective consciousness and selfhood, it cannot banish the ineffable element of our encounter with beauty, nature, art, other people, or the transcendent, "the beyond beyond all beyondering."

Chapter 4

Religion

When I was six years old I constructed out of paper an "odometer," a device with paper wheels encircling a paper core, and on each wheel I wrote the numbers 0 to 9, thus recreating a car's odometer. Furtively, under my desk at school, I would spin the wheels of my odometer, turning the wheel farthest to the right from 0 to 9, and then advancing the next wheel from 0 to 1, and repeating, advancing the second wheel to 2, and so forth. But my purpose was not to record mileage. Rather, by gradually advancing, through these finite steps, from easily comprehensible numbers—numbers that corresponded to my tangible experience of the world—to unimaginably high numbers, my little machine, created with my own hands, allowed me to travel, step by step, from my mundane, finite world to ineffable, numinous transcendence—"from the familiar and tangible to the mystic realm" (E. O. Wilson, *supra*). Although I was much too young to articulate this, that's how it *felt* at the time.

Our early ancestors did not need to look far to encounter the numinous (nor did they need odometers to do so!). Ineffable mystery presented itself everywhere. Metaphorically, as Fromm and Jeffers suggest, they had left the Garden of Eden and found themselves in a world that was at once natural and daimonic. Animals, and the manifold aspects of the natural environment, seemed to possess human-like consciousness and intentional agency.[1] Even stones, as Karen Armstrong (*A Short History of Myth*) observes, "embodied strength, permanence, solidity and an absolute mode of being that was quite different from the human state."[2] She cites also the regenerative powers of trees and other plants, and of the moon.

Ritual practices emerged in an effort to appease the daimons of the natural world and to incorporate into oneself the desired qualities seen to reside therein. Over time, though, the divine mysteries of the visible world began to fade. The gods, still numerous, dwelt out of sight, in high places or in the sea, until at last they too lost their hold. "Thunder is no longer the voice of an angry god, nor is lightning his avenging missile," says Jung. "No river contains his spirit, no tree is the life principle of a man, no snake the embodiment of wisdom, no mountain cave the home of a great demon. No voices now speak to man from stones, plants, and animals, nor does he speak to them believing that they can hear."[3] Eventually, the notion of a single, transcendent power and glory, beyond human reach and ken, came to dominate the religious imagination and belief of much of the world. Even for us nonbelievers, as my odometer illustrates, the imagination will not allow itself to be bound by the horizon of the perceptible world.

The sense of the incomprehensible transcendent is primordial in the human species. As Mircea Eliade (*The Sacred and the Profane*) explains, "The phenomenon of the remoteness of the supreme god is already documented on the archaic levels of culture."[4] The sense of an overarching transcendence was not born in Biblical times but in the early development of human consciousness. The prehistoric humans who experienced the sacred in their natural, accessible surroundings experienced it also in the limitless sky, which reminded them that there is more to reality than we can ever see or grasp. Karen Armstrong, citing the thought and research of Eliade and of Rudolf Otto, observes, "The sky towered above them, inconceivably immense, inaccessible and eternal. It was the very essence of transcendence and otherness. ... It was by its very nature numinous. ..."[5]

Whatever the physicists and cosmologists may tell us, it is impossible for the human imagination to conceive of limits to space or time. Thus, infinity and eternity, those unfathomable *noumena*, are also *numena*; they work their emotional magic through powerful metaphors: the sea, the sky, the starry heavens.

This sense of a boundless reality that overarches the tangible, visible, accessible world surely would have been a seminal inspiration for the religious imagination. According to Ernst Cassirer (*Language and Myth*), citing the work of various scholars, the religious imagination began not with individual deities, animistic or otherwise, but with a generalized notion of a power, or holiness (cf. Eliade's notion of the sacred), separate from the ordinary, the mundane, the profane. This quality, or force, is manifested in certain persons, animals, and things. In the next stage of religious development, "momentary deities" appear.

As culture progressed, these momentary gods were replaced by "a new series of divinities, originating not from spontaneous feelings but from the ordered and continual activities of mankind."[6] These "special gods" were associated with specific, ongoing human activities. At a later stage, the gods began to acquire *personality*. Eventually these various personal gods fused into a single god.

In the early stages of monotheism, as Cassirer explains, the personality and power of God was inextricably bound to his name. This was true not only of the God of Abraham but also of gods in other civilizations. God was synonymous with the Word. Thus, in Genesis, God—the Word—said, "Let there be light!" And (by the pure agency of his word), there was light.

But when we come to Exodus, it appears that something new is happening. Moses, having been addressed by God from the burning bush and instructed to prepare the Israelites for their flight from Egypt, asked God, "When the people ask who has sent me, who shall I say has sent me?" God replied, "I am that I am. Tell the children of Israel that 'I Am' has sent you."[7] Now, rather than having a name—and thus being, as it were, a personality subject to description—God is to be nameless and thus recognized as being beyond all human powers of description and comprehension. At some point it became taboo to speak or to spell out God's name.

But the human spirit is not content to allow ultimate transcendence to remain so inaccessible (as my childhood odometer signified!). And so, in the Gospel of John, "the Word became flesh and dwelt among us, full of grace and truth."[8] We finite, imperfect mortals are joined with the infinite, the perfect, the incomprehensible, the transcendent—the sacred, in Eliade's terms.

Claude Lévy-Strauss points out that in myth as also in music the main theme recurs in variations. Thus, when Jesus at the Last Supper says "Take, eat! This is my body, this is my blood of the New Testament,"[9] we see the original theme ("the Word became flesh and dwelt among us") restated: the Word as flesh will no longer dwell among us but will return to Heaven, i.e., to transcendence, but through the Eucharist (the ingestion of the bread and wine) we will partake of the Word. The union of transcendent Word and mortal flesh will be preserved.

Jung, Campbell, and others have extensively explored the ways in which myths and religious stories speak to deep psychological truths. What Picasso said of art can be said, as well, of myth: it is the lie that reveals the truth. Myths speak eloquently of our human need to feel joined in some way not only with the world and our fellow humans but with the infinite and eternal, the numinously transcendent, beyond the reaches of perception and of science. Even Confucianism, with its humanistic, this-worldly emphasis, is not without this sense of transcendence; for its adherents, Heaven is that intuition of perfection toward which human effort must be aimed and of which ritual practices are a reminder and a reinforcement.

The power of religious language to touch the souls of even us unbelievers was revealed to me one evening around

Christmastime many years ago. As I listened to some of the music from Handel's *Messiah*, my atheist heart was deeply moved by those familiar, beautifully sung words: *I know that my Redeemer liveth*. Only belatedly did I learn that this very Christian-sounding statement was uttered not by one of the apostles, nor by Isaiah foretelling the coming of the Messiah, but by Job, who, out of the depths of his despair, was able to speak these poignant words of faith. I suspect that most men and women, whether religious believers or not, can relate on some deep level with these powerful words. Whether in hope or despair, we are joined with our fellow humanity in a shared world of meaning and aspiration. The Redeemer is not a guarantor of success but the Thou of true relation, "a presence by means of which we are told that nevertheless there is meaning."[10]

One might assume that religion's powerful hold on humanity stems from the solace it provides in the face of death, of feelings of guilt or unworthiness, and of the prevalence of evil and suffering. Religion also provides a powerful sense of community, a community of fellow believers. Certainly religion has these functions, perhaps for most people past and present. But Jung, at least, was convinced that the great religious stories, whether of the Bible or of other traditions, were not concocted, as it were, to quell people's anxieties or even to wield sacerdotal power (although John Dominic Crossan, recounting the development of the early Church, notes that cynical power-mongering played a role). Rather, these stories spring from deeper wells, expressing needs and hopes relating to meaning, duality, transcendence. Clothed in the language of myth and metaphor, they speak to us across the ages, even to those of us who don't take them literally. Crossan is right in saying that the deeper truths of religious stories are revealed when we see their language as "connotative" (figurative) rather than "denotative" (literal). Crossan reminds us that Jesus himself understood that religious discourse requires figurative language; throughout his ministry he used parable and figuration, even to the point of challenging his hearers' comprehension at times.

My parents, both born Methodist, found their way to the more theologically liberal Religious Society of Friends (Quakers), and I was reared in that denomination. Howard Brinton, in his history of Quakerism (*Friends for 300 Years*), reminds us that from the first meetings of that religious society in the mid-1600s, "Friends" (Quakers), rejecting the liturgical trappings of traditional religion, found it useful and indeed necessary to have recourse to figurative language. Thus, for instance, "the Light" and "the Seed" became commonly used terms in Quaker vocabulary. For Friends (Quakers) then and now, such terms capture some of the ineffable numinosity that Rudolf Otto expostulated. By thus expressing, connotatively, the foundational discernments of the sect, they become a call to action in the world.

The story of Jesus at Bethany[11] is a story as moving as any as a statement of basic human need and, in a sense, a prescription for action. According to this story, Jesus arrives at the home of Lazarus and his sisters, Mary and Martha, accompanied by some of his disciples, including Judas Iscariot, who would later betray him. Jesus is sitting at the table while Martha is preparing a meal for all of them. Mary takes oil and anoints Jesus with it. Martha remonstrates that Mary should be helping her with the meal instead of pouring oil on Jesus.[12] Judas also remonstrates, saying that the oil is expensive; it could have been sold and the money given to the poor. But Jesus answers them both, saying, "What Mary has done is an act of love. The poor you will always have with you, but soon I will not be with you." He reminds them that anointment is a preparation for burial. And so Jesus needed to feel, before he died, that he was loved. Prior to the start of his ministry, he had been baptized by John the Baptist, who had declared him *ha-mashiach*—the Messiah. The Romans would derisively call him *Rex Iudorum*—King of the Jews. But by this simple act of kindness and recognition at the hands of an ordinary woman, he became χριστός *(khristos)*, the Anointed.

In Homer *(The Odyssey)*, we see anointment as a gesture of hospitality—performed by a female member of the household— toward an honored guest. Mary's anointment of Jesus had this aspect, which does not, I think, negate the additional metaphorical power of Jesus' presentiment of burial nor of Jesus as *khristos*.

An interesting—if only partial—parallel might be seen here. The anointed one in the *Odyssey* is Odysseus' son, Telemachus— the Son, if you will. He travels the real world of mortal humans in search of information about his father, and is anointed by mortal humans. Odysseus, meanwhile—the Father—is wandering through a supernatural world of demigods, nymphs, monsters, etc., a world that he alone survives. Father and son are eventually reunited. The wicked perish. The righteous king reigns.

In the Old Testament, anointment was associated with, or was an equivalent of, coronation, and in the TV series *The Crown*,[13] we see that ritual re-enacted in modern times. During the coronation of Elizabeth II, the young queen is anointed by the Archbishop of Canterbury, who says, "Even as Nathan the Prophet anointed Solomon the king, so do I, Archbishop of Canterbury, anoint you, Elizabeth, Queen of England." Her resentful, uninvited uncle, the Duke of Windsor,[14] is watching this on TV with his wife and a roomful of friends in Paris. An American voice is heard in the back of the room: "Aw, this is just a bunch of silly pageantry." But the Duke turns to him and says, "Oh no it's not. It's magic!"

And that is the point of anointment, whether the anointed one is a monarch being crowned, a prophet being hailed as the Christ, or ourselves, figuratively anointed by a word or act from someone who recognizes us as special and of worth. It's magic. The Greeks had a word for this, too: χάρις *(kharis)*, which means gift, usually in the sense of a divinely bestowed gift. A person blessed with such a gift possesses the quality of χάρισμα (*kharisma*).

Who among us has never wished that we possessed charisma, and who among us has not admired and envied those who do? Here, of course, we speak of more than the gift of life and of whatever easily describable attributes we may possess, but of that special something—what John Potts, in his *A History of Charisma*, calls a mysterious, elusive quality. This definition of charisma, even as it is used today in secular contexts, is traceable, as Potts explains, back to the Greek origins and religious history of the word. The apostle Paul (who wrote in Greek) used the word in his letters to the Corinthians. Paul contrasts "charismata" (plural of "charisma") with "pneumatika" (spiritual gifts); these latter were claimed by the elite of the Christian community at Corinth. Paul felt that the building of a vital, sustainable and sustaining community required, instead, "charismata," divinely bestowed gifts of various kinds that were available to elite and non-elite alike and would serve to build community rather than to aggrandize elite individuals. But in the ensuing centuries, as the Church became a hierarchical institution with set creeds and dogmas, the notion of charismata fell into disfavor and disuse. In the early twentieth century, German sociologist Max Weber revived the word "charisma," but in a somewhat new context, namely, leadership, political and otherwise. But Weber's use of the word retained the notion of an innate gift and took on something of the "mysterious, elusive" quality that we associate with charisma today. As the twentieth century continued, the word was used in two very different contexts and meanings. On the one hand, the religious meaning of the word was revived as "charismatic" groups and individuals emerged among Catholic and Protestant communities. The Pauline charismata of prophesy and glossolalia (speaking in tongues) were revived, but as Potts notes disapprovingly, these latter-day charismatics missed the mark. For Paul, prophesy was a matter of divinely inspired illumination and ministry, not a claim to be able to predict future events. As for glossolalia, Paul ranked this as the lowest of the charismata, and, more to the point, he urged that people who speak in tongues (i.e., gibberish) would do well to provide intelligible interpretation. And again, for Paul community-building and edification, not individual aggrandizement, were the goals. Meanwhile, a totally secular use of the word "charisma" became increasingly widespread during the course of the past century; the word was applied not only to political leaders, notably Kennedy, but to film stars and other celebrities, as well as to noncelebrities among us who appear to be gifted with "that certain something." In all of these usages, the notion of a mysterious gift has remained.

I first heard the word "charisma" in my youth when John F. Kennedy was running for President. Certainly Kennedy had many gifts that were neither mysterious nor elusive: he was wealthy, good-looking, and charming; he was a war hero and a Pulitzer-Prize-winning author; he had a glamorous wife and a glamorous life. But he seemed to have something more than glamour and good fortune. He seemed to have charisma. But can charisma be found in the absence of fame, physical attractiveness, personal charm, social status, eloquent speech, or talent for leadership and inspiration? Is notable achievement required? Does one have to be "cool"? Is it a quality that can be cultivated? As Potts asks in conclusion: "Can it be rationally dissected and satisfactorily explained, or is it the result of some inner gift?"[15]

If charisma does, in fact, have the quality of mystery and elusiveness, it would seem that there is something of the numinous here—the qualities of "grace," of "beyond the usual," and even of the "wholly other" that Rudolf Otto expounded. But does that mean that we ordinary folk are unqualified to possess charisma? Or are we, like Paul's Corinthians, worthy of receiving the *kharismata*, regardless of our station or status?

I will resist any temptation to give a facile and comforting answer. We do not all have equal gifts and we are not all equally charismatic (in the secular sense, at least). Although there is, no doubt, an ineffable quality in the charismatic personality, it cannot be denied that physical attractiveness, especially of a distinctive kind, can go a long way. And fame! Who among us has never wished for fame? Whose pulse has not quickened at the sight or touch of a truly famous person? A famous person is not just a person but a *personage* and a *numen*. However much we may try to deny it, the famous person, known to millions whom he or she will never know, lives on a different plane. To borrow the language of Sartre and the existentialists, we are *existents*; they, the famous, are *beings*. Mere persons exist in their surroundings; personages—the famous—have being in the world at large. They are, as we say, larger than life. In the presence of the numinous personage, famous and/or charismatic, we feel our own being somehow increased. There are mythic parallels here: in the medieval mind, the king's touch had the power to heal, as did Jesus' touch in the minds of his worshipers. We do not expect to be healed by the touch of Tom Hanks or Nicole Kidman, but through their *being* we are lifted, to some small degree, above mere existence. Nonsense, you say? Try to imagine a world in which there were no famous people—a world not unlike a world with no human characters in novels, stories, plays, movies, or operas.

But you would be rightly critical if I were to propose to end the story here. I am not suggesting that we must either become famous or abandon all hope for meaningful life, nor am I proposing that famous people are necessarily better than the rest of us. Nor do physical attractiveness and charisma necessarily go hand in hand; one can have one without the other. As for the notion of being a "personage," Spanish philosopher José Ortega y Gasset shows us that it's not necessary to be famous to be a personage, as opposed to a mere person. All human beings are persons by definition. But to be a personage is to authentically *choose*, and to realize "our vocation, our vital program, our 'entelechy'."[16] In other words, to choose to *be*.

Jean-Paul Sartre explores the duality of *existing* and *being* in his short novel *Nausea*. The protagonist, Roquentin, is a thirty-year-old historian working on a scholarly biography in a French town called Bouville (surely not coincidentally, the French word *boue* means "mud"). During the course of everyday activities, Roquentin, unaware of existentialist philosophy, nevertheless finds himself experiencing the disconcerting difference between "essence" and "existence." During a visit to a city park, trees and rocks and so forth lose their essences and become raw existence—mere facticity. At the same time, Roquentin's own self likewise becomes mere existence—*de trop* (unnecessary excess)— "All the things around me were made of the same material as I. ..."[17] Words, the medium through which we describe the objects of our world and express their meaning for us, fall away, and everything runs together in a disgusting, viscous ooze.

In the absence of meaningful, sense-giving, emotionally laden encounter between self and world (i.e., non-self), there is a painful sense of collapse and despair, such as we experience in deep depression. In such a state, even the mundane pleasure we normally experience in eating tasty food disappears. If circumstances require us to interact with family or friends or others, we feel forced, as it were, to pretend; any interaction whatsoever feels like a pretense. In my own case (many decades ago), I came out of a deep depression when I made myself go to a movie. During the course of the movie (it happened to be *Faces* by John Cassavetes) I felt engaged by the characters, and when I walked out of the theater after the movie, all of my real-world problems were still there, but I was back in the world—a world of meaning. For Roquentin, his return comes when he drops in at a bistro one evening and hears a woman singing a blues song on the jukebox. But he experiences something even more than a return to the everyday world of meaning: he experiences the numinous. As Sartre puts it, Roquentin experiences the music—and its composer and singer—as *being*, as essence. "And I, too, wanted to *be*."[18]

Thus, a three-tiered possibility for human existence is revealed. In deep depression, and in Roquentin's experience in the park, everything, including ourselves, loses meaning. The color and warmth and likes and dislikes and passions of our normal life fade to grey. We feel disconnected, disengaged, lost, meaningless. Here there is no encounter, no project, no hope. In our normal, everyday state, however, the people and things and nature around us have meaning and, to a greater or lesser degree, emotional resonance for us. We have projects. But "normal" is not enough for us—interesting and rewarding, perhaps, but temporal, finite, never quite adequate to the fullness of hope and expectation. Here we are in what Eliade calls the secular world. As both Eliade and Sartre tell us, we want *being*.

Sartre and Eliade, each in his own way, show us that we are rooted in existence, in a world the components of which can be seen, heard, touched, examined, used, judged. And we ourselves are part of that world; we are among those components. But virtually any of these components—a thing, a sequence of sounds or arrangement of colors, an animal, a human person—can become what Eliade calls a homology.[19] A homology remains what it is in its actual existence, but to the human imagination and emotion, it takes on *being*. As Sartre's Roquentin tells us, *being* is "beyond"; "behind the existence which falls from one present to the other... and slip[s] towards death."[20] For Eliade, citing Rudolf Otto (*The Idea of the Holy*), *being* is "the wholly other," the *numen*, the *mysterium fascinans* beyond denotative description. But we cannot reach this numinous *being* apart from our concrete, existential surroundings—Buber's "lived concrete"—the only possible origin, as Yeats reminds us,[21] of our "masterful images" of "pure mind."

Sartre's use of a piece of music to illustrate his main point seems particularly apt. When I go to the supermarket or the gym, there is usually a radio broadcasting popular music. Most of the songs are familiar; the songs I particularly like may not be the ones that you particularly like, but in general, these familiar songs have withstood the test of time. Occasionally, new songs are heard. All too often, these untested songs sound pathetically contrived. One can imagine the composer desperately (or perhaps lackadaisically) trying to come up with something. These songs lack *being*; their puny existence is, as Sartre would say, "*de trop*" (useless excess). But some new songs have the elusive quality of the enduring songs: they seem somehow *necessary*: how could we have lived fully, *as me*, without them? They have *being*. Through them, we feel our own being enhanced.

When I was five years old — almost six — I attended some sort of Christmas program with my family. The only thing I recall from that program is that at one point an enlarged image of the then-current 1950 Christmas seal (to raise money to fight tuberculosis) was projected on a screen. It had a green and red background, and angel singers rendered in golden hues. It was only a stamp, not a gorgeous sunset or the Grand Canyon or moonrise over the sea, nor was it a wondrous work of art or design. Yet somehow that seal became for me a homology: mundane existence was imbued with emotional power. Here was *being*. Can it be rationally explained? I don't know, but I suspect that most people, past and present, have had such homologies. Blessed are those who have such experiences not only in childhood but in maturity.

This homologous, or numinous, encounter with a Christmas seal — an imaginatively created object— is perhaps somewhere between the encounter with objects or aspects of nature and the encounter with art. But in all of these encounters, numinous being is experienced. As Jung put it: "... the matter-of-fact and the commonplace come to wear an altered countenance, and can even acquire a new glamour..."[22]

There is a powerful tendency among individuals and cultures to deny our individual otherness—to deny what Fromm recognized as our radical separateness and what I, as a small child, recognized when my imagination placed me in a little helicopter. Entire worldviews are based on the notion of "cosmic unity," that we are all one, that everything is one, and that all dualities are illusions that disappear when one reaches "enlightenment." Certainly this worldview has two major elements of truth: first, there is only one nature, and we (as a species), along with everything else in the universe, are part of it. And second, I cannot exist, as a human subject, in any other mode than "in the world"—I cannot exist in a vat or vacuum. "No man is an island." But we've seen that each human individual is in the world not as an indistinguishable part thereof but as "wholly other." If this were not so, and if the dualities of human experience were mere chimera, there could be no encounter, no meeting of I and Thou (because, in fact, there would be no "I" and no "Thou"), no grandness of the Grand Canyon, no love, erotic or otherwise, and no true art.

Moreover, biology teaches us that every living organism can persist in existence only by setting itself off from its surroundings. Otherwise, it succumbs to entropy and death. All life is individual, however dependent we may be on the surrounding world. I am dependent upon the world, but the world and I are not—and cannot be—one and the same.

It has been argued that the kinds of issues I've been discussing are not as universal as we in the West are wont to think, and that our notions of "the human condition" are Western conceits. It is commonly assumed that notions of immutable duality—including those of self and other, self and world, self and the transcendent—are peculiarly Western, and that non-Western cultures are essentially monistic in the sense that all is essentially one, and each of us is as one with the universe and with transcendent being, even if it takes years of meditation and/or lifetimes of *samsara* to reach the enlightenment of *nirvana*. But as Huston Smith points out in his *World's Religions* and in other writings, without minimizing the differences between Western and non-Western cultures and religious outlook, religions around the world recognize these dualities. To some measure and in at least some quarters, they recognize that there can be no real encounter, and no real love, between entities that are one—that are in a state of complete unity. Smith quotes a sixteenth-century Hindu philosopher and poet, Tukaram, who urged his readers and followers to "Pray no more for utter oneness with God," for "Where were the joy, if the two were one?"[23] Hinduism, in fact, recognizes that human individuals are unique and non-interchangeable; what works, spiritually, for one may not work for another. There are many yogas.[24] Buddhism provides a similar recognition. And in the Islamic tradition, Smith quotes Muhammad Iqbal: "This inexplicable finite centre of experience is the fundamental fact of the universe. All life is individual; there is no such thing as universal life."[25] Bringing it back to the West, Campbell asserts that "The goal of Western religions is not to bring about a sense of identity with the transcendent. Their goal is to bring about a *relationship* [emphasis added] between human beings and God."[26]

By contrast, two eloquent and charismatic spokesmen for the monistic viewpoint achieved widespread popularity during the last century. The British-American Alan Watts and the Indian Krishnamurti urged us to give full attention to the experience of the present moment. Both men were deeply appreciative of the beauty of nature and concerned for its preservation. Many passages in Krishnamurti's writings invite us to experience with him the quiet joys of nature's beauty as he walks country roads, beaches, river banks, mountains and valleys at various times of day. And Watts (*The Wisdom of Insecurity*) repeatedly insists on the primacy of the present moment. "We know no

other moment than the present moment. It is always dying...
yet at the same time it is always being born."[27] Our memory
of the past and our anticipation of the future can exist only
as *present* experience; we can have no direct experience of the
past, which is gone, or the future, which is yet to come, and
unknowable. Thus, according to Watts, if I think that "I" exist
as a thing apart, I am in a state of illusion. "No one ever found
an 'I' apart from some present experience, or some experience
apart from an 'I'—which is only to say that the two are the same
thing." And: "You do not *have* a sensation of the sky; you *are*
that sensation... There is no 'you' apart from what you sense,
feel, and know. This is why the mystics and many of the poets
give frequent utterance to the feeling that they are 'one with the
All' or 'united with God' ..."[28]

Krishnamurti (*All the Marvelous Earth*) expresses a similar
outlook: "What is beauty? ... What takes place when you look
at something which is actually marvelously beautiful: a statue,
a poem, a lily in the pond, or a well-kept lawn? At that moment,
the very majesty of a mountain makes you forget yourself. Have
you ever been in that position? If you have, you have seen that
then you don't exist, only that grandeur exists."[29]

More currently, psychologist Susan Blackmore
(*Consciousness*), like Watts and Krishnamurti, asserts that there
is *experience*, but no *experiencer*. She holds out the hope that with
lots of hard work—Zen meditation or similar disciplines—we
may rid ourselves of the "illusions" of a continuous self and of
other selves, and reach "a state in which phenomena rise and
fall away but without any sense of time or place, and with no
one experiencing them."[30]

It seems to me that we have already seen the fallacy of this
viewpoint, however enticing it may be. Krishnamurti is right
in saying that in the moment of what we might call numinous
experience, we forget ourselves and our mundane concerns. But
is there not some irony in his asking us to *recall* such moments?

He is right in saying (elsewhere) that "All of life is relationship. To be is to be related—otherwise you have no existence."[31] Here he appears largely to agree with Buber,[32] to which I say "Amen!" But there surely has to be an "I" if there is to be a relationship with a "Thou." Similarly, Watts is correct in his assertion that there is no "I" without experience of the world. But my "I," my self, cannot be utterly reduced to the moment of present experience. Even in the presence of the numinous "wholly other," the self—the embodied experiencer—resonates with memory and imagination. Experience is in the moment (or, as some have called it, "the extended present"[33]), but memories of past experiences come to mind, and thus become (in altered form) present experience.

British neurologist Raymond Tallis quotes Hume, whose empiricism prefigured Watts, Krishnamurti, and Blackmore by at least a couple of centuries: "There are some philosophers who imagine we are every moment intimately conscious of what we call our *self*. ... For my part, when I enter most intimately into what I call *myself*, I always stumble on some particular perception or other, of heat or cold, light or shade, love or hatred, pain or pleasure. I can never catch *myself* at any time without a perception and can never observe but the perception."

But Tallis replies: "[T]hose perceptions... had a common ownership that allowed the owner—one David Hume—to claim them as his own and, because of this, to be able to access them *in a way no one else could* [my emphasis]."[34]

In their laudable emphasis on the experience of the present moment, Watts and Krishnamurti, as well as Blackmore, appear to ignore the fact that each of our present moments is enriched by the contributions and reverberations of memory, as well as of future possibility and imagination. The fact that our memories are unreliable as to objective accuracy, or that our future is speculative and factually unknown, does not obviate those contributions and reverberations. Steven Johnson, in a *New York*

Times Magazine article, cites PET-scan research showing that even when our minds are seemingly at rest rather than engaged in focused effort, our minds are, in fact, very much engaged with the past and the future—and this is not a bad thing. "A growing number of scholars, drawn from a wide swath of disciplines—neuroscience, philosophy, computer science—now argue that this aptitude for cognitive time travel... may be the defining property of human intelligence. ... What gave flight to the human mind and all its inventiveness... may... have been freeing our minds from the tyranny of the present."[35]

And given that my memories are mine alone—not yours or anyone else's—the notion that I, as a self, don't exist, or that "I" and my present experience are the same thing, doesn't hold up. As Muhammad Iqbal said, "... the thread of continuity in the life of the self is furnished by memory..."

In arguing against monism, I am not arguing in favor of a Cartesian mind-body substance dualism. I am arguing for authentic encounter—an I-and-Thou encounter with the as-yet undisclosed (to use Buber's eloquent phraseology). If there is no I, how can there be a Thou? I and Thou exist in the present moment, but also in time—past and future.

From earliest times, human life has involved ritual, an effort to connect our earthly existence and exigencies with the numinous, the powerful, the transcendent. As Newberg et al. (*Why God Won't Go Away*) have said, "... the ceremonial rites of all human societies, from the most primitive to the most exalted, are an elaboration of the neurobiological need... to escape the limiting boundaries of the self."[36] And as Karen Armstrong says, "If a myth does not enable people to participate in the sacred in some way, it becomes remote and fades from their consciousness."[37] Even in our modern civilizations, ritual has its place, even in secular contexts, particularly those involving marriage, death, and the legitimacy of state authority (judicial robes are an example). Why? Because these events or institutions are not a mere matter of course, to be accepted unproblematically. The acceptance of these events or institutions are enhanced by ritual, by linking them to a tradition and to transcendent reality, and to a community that accepts that reality.

My wife and I once attended a coming-of-age ceremony on the Mescalero Apache reservation in New Mexico. Two girls, having reached puberty, were the focus of this ceremony. In addition to the girls' own participation, which took place inside a tepee, male dancers danced around a bonfire nearby. The "crown dancers," resplendent in headdresses and garb emblazoned with traditional symbols, embodied what we might call the Apollonian, rational, well-ordered cosmology of the Mescalero Apache people. But dancing with the crown dancers were two or three "clowns." Their outfits lacked the traditional symbols and well-ordered majesty of the crown dancers, and even incorporated mundane commercial elements from the surrounding white culture. They remind us that human life and experience is not entirely well-ordered and rational; that there is a nonrational, Dionysian side that must be accommodated in our lives. Additionally—and even more strikingly—the duality of the crown dancers and the clowns can be seen as the duality of the sacred and the profane—we live in both worlds.[38]

Martin Buber addressed this aspect of community, observing that a community (e.g., a religious community) retains its vitality so long as its members retain a meaningful connection to, and experience of, the "original relational event."[39] The beliefs and practices of the community may evolve over time, but the originating event points to an epiphany—or what Eliade calls a hierophany, a disclosure of the sacred—an encounter with transcendence that resonates across the years, a flame that is rekindled in the hearts of succeeding generations and lights their efforts in the world. As Karen Armstrong says, "A myth demands action."[40]

Some people have argued that the world would be better off without religion, given the fanaticism and intolerance that it has too often generated. But religion in some form will always be with us, and rightly so. As Raymond Tallis says, "Religion addresses hungers that are shared by believers and infidels alike."[41] The Apollonian disciplines of science and philosophy, and even the Apollonian-Dionysian activity of art, indispensable though they are, cannot encompass all of human experience. Religious metaphor goes where science—and even art—cannot go: into the dark recesses of our encounter with mystery and transcendence, and brings us back out into our temporal, uncertain world with renewed strength. The grandeur of Michelangelo's Sistine Chapel ceiling is not that it recreates God in all his glory—either as myth or as reality—but that it bodies forth our experience of longing and imagination and transcendence. With beauty and power, it asserts the human spirit over raw existence.

Chapter 5

Death

As this book is about the human condition in the light of subjective consciousness, it seems fitting to devote some discussion to an inescapable aspect thereof, an aspect that the existentialists—notably Heidegger—characterized as "being towards death." Many animals, including humans, experience fear, but only humans are able to experience *dread*; only humans are able to look to an unseen future and reflect on death and its inevitability. It may well be that most of us—even those of us who are "senior citizens," and those of us who disbelieve in immortality—do not spend much time wallowing in dread of death, although that can change with cruel abruptness. Throughout our lives our inexorable fate lurks in the shadows, behind the bright sheen of our normal, meaningful, and often enjoyable lives. But perhaps no other aspect of our condition points as starkly to the duality of human experience. Although our unbounded imagination flies to the infinite, the eternal, the morally perfect, and the numinously beautiful and meaningful, we know that our knowledge will always be limited, our moral standing will always fall short, and our lives, however blessed by God's or fate's grace, will never attain the fullness of numinosity and meaning that we might long for. However wonderful the gift of life, there will always be an incompleteness, a shortfall. And above all, we know that we whose imagination soars to timelessness are, in fact, living in bounded time, and that our individual life in this world will someday come to an end.

Western religions, with their notions of Heaven and Hell, have sought to provide both the hope of eternal life (even if this hope is of much less central focus for some individuals and religious communities than for others) and also the satisfying notion that the good will be rewarded and the evil punished. The Eastern religions (e.g., Hinduism) also address this human desire for everlasting life and for justice, though in a somewhat different way. The soul is seen as subject to reincarnation, based on the principle of karma. A life well-lived, and in accordance with ethical norms, deserves a favorable reincarnation. The eventual goal is nirvana — unity with the divine.

The notion that my consciousness will somehow survive my death and that I will end up in Heaven (and where might Heaven be?), or somewhere else, is completely incompatible with science and reason — it's impossible to even think about how this could actually occur. As Raymond Tallis says, "There is no account of the afterlife that is imaginable, never mind attractive, for all that it is often a source of consolation..."[1] You might ask why, given the fact that I view my experience of this particular self as a mystery, can I not also simply accept life after death as a mysterious but possible reality? I see the two matters as quite different species, so to speak — as apples and oranges, if you will. I find myself experiencing just this self rather than any other, and (like Pascal as well as many others in our own time) I'm unable to find any reason for this; the matter appears to be beyond the scope of science or reason. I'm not at all suggesting that this is a "divine" or supernatural mystery, but simply that it's a mystery, *tout court* — the mystery of subjective consciousness. But as for life after death, I have no experience or observation of any such thing. Moreover, as stated earlier, although science does not explain why I am just this self, it does appear to demonstrate that living, functioning neuroanatomy and physiology is required for consciousness, including consciousness of self, to occur.

Similarly, with regard to reincarnation, I can imagine no process by which a "soul," conceived of as subjective consciousness, could leap, as it were, from one body to another. I'm aware that even in the West some people believe, or have an intuition, that they had a previous life. Not surprisingly, these imagined previous lives are never thought to have been commonplace; inevitably, they were lives of glamour and/ or historical significance. After all, why bother imagining a previous life if that life was completely ordinary, or if it fails to add meaning of some sort to this present life?

But might there not be a sort of reincarnation, even in a completely non-supernatural world? If there is no reason why *I* am here (remember: there are plenty of reasons why there is *a person* here, but not why this person is *me*), there would appear to be no reason why, after this life has ended, "I" might not find myself in some new life—another person, or perhaps even a nonhuman animal—coping as best as he or she can with another set of circumstances in another time and place. But of course this new "I" would be a wholly different "I" and would have no connection whatsoever with my present "I": any connection would be impossible. Thus, there would be no memory of this life, and therefore no regret if I find myself in less fortunate—or even nonhuman—circumstances. In any case, we are back to our original situation: this current life will come to an end. What are we to make of this state of affairs?

Some people have tried to find solace in the thought that some aspect of their existence will survive death—their progeny,[2] their good works and achievements, or their influence on the next generation, their community, or the world at large, "concentrating on the welfare of those who will survive you and on the success of projects or causes you care about," as Thomas Nagel says.[3] But he concedes that this can be only a partial consolation. Perhaps there will be the satisfaction of looking back on a life well and fully lived. Some other attempts at consolation I've encountered fall far short of the mark, including a notion I came across to the effect that I can find solace in the thought of the atoms that make up my body dispersing after my death and constituting new entities, including other humans. Sorry! That does nothing for me. I do not identify myself with the atoms of my body, or anything or anyone they might later reconstitute themselves as. I am a unique, subjective consciousness in the world—I am, in fact, *me*—and when I die, I will no longer be me. Woody Allen famously summed up the shortcomings of all attempts to evade the tragedy of one's own demise: "I don't want to be immortal through my works; I want to be immortal by not dying."

The Spanish writer Miguel de Unamuno (*Tragic Sense of Life*) was deeply troubled by the inevitability of death. He found solace in his Catholic faith, which promises eternal life for the faithful in Jesus Christ. This was hardly surprising; as Unamuno himself acknowledged, being a Spaniard and being a Catholic are, at least historically and in his day, so closely intertwined. But Unamuno recognized two things: first, that despite the rationalist tradition in Catholic apologetics from Thomas Aquinas on down, the fact is that neither reason nor science supports Catholic belief; only faith can do that—and that was good enough for Unamuno. More crucially, Unamuno recognized this also: Christian faith (like other faiths) offers, to its believers, the hope of life everlasting, *but not on this earth*, our home, the scene of all our loves and joys and sorrows and projects and aspirations. Hence the tragic sense of life, even for a believer like Unamuno.

But Unamuno had some advice for us to live by while we're still here. "Our greatest endeavor must be to make ourselves irreplaceable; ... to make... the fact... that no one else can fill the gap that will be left when we die a practical truth."[4] This endeavor is not always easily achieved, as indicated by Vincent van Gogh's desperate question: "What is it that I can do?" I can even relate, to a degree, with Kafka's "Hunger Artist," who starved himself to death, not in order to impress people, as his audiences assumed, but because he found no food that he liked enough to eat. Given the fact that we are mysteriously and absurdly thrown into our little time and space in all of infinity and eternity, the aspiration to be irreplaceable—to fill a gap—is perfectly natural. Because we want to be larger than death, it is only natural that we long to be larger than life, to possess *kharisma*, to be, somehow, numinous, and not mere conscious matter, a subject to ourselves and a mere object to others. Like Sartre's Roquentin, we want to *be*.

There is also this consolation in the face of our mortality: Most people, whether they believe in an afterlife or not, go through at least two stages toward the end. There is a stage of reluctance, even desperation, at the thought of death. Many people, while they are still in reasonably good health, believe that when the ravages of old age, disability, and ill-health overtake them, they will be ready to go. But when they at last find themselves in that condition, they find that it's not so simple; the reluctance is there, not so much a reluctance to leave a life of hopeless decrepitude as to *leave this world*. And of course there are the tragic instances of life cut abruptly short by accident, homicide, suicide, or war. Mercifully, though, for perhaps most people there seems to come, at some point, a more or less stoic acceptance. Dylan Thomas may have wanted his father to "rage against the dying of the light," but many—perhaps most—seem to find more peace than rage at the end. This acceptance of death has been observed not only in the very old, dying of natural causes, but sometimes even in the young, mortally wounded, for instance, on the field of battle.[5]

Activists and homesteaders Scott and Helen Nearing (whom I was privileged to know through my parents, who were among their friends) wrote a book called *Living the Good Life*. Some years after Scott's death at the age of 100, Helen wrote *Loving and Leaving the Good Life*.[6] Reflecting on deep old age and the approach of death, Helen wrote: "I was finally experiencing old age and finding it not without compensations. One can savor sights and sounds more deeply when one gets really old. It may be the last time you see a sunset, a tree, the snow, or know winter. The sea, the lake—all become, as in childhood, magical and a great wonder, then seen for the first time, now perhaps for the last. Music, bird songs, the wind, the waves: one listens to tones with deeper delight and appreciation—'loving well,' to borrow Shakespeare's seventy-third sonnet, 'that which I must leave ere long.'"

This brings us to the question of death in poetic imagery—the effort, as André Malraux said, "to deny our nothingness"[7] through our own creative response. As with beauty, art, religious experience, consciousness, and life itself, ordinary language is inadequate in the face of life's end. The human spirit naturally turns to myth and metaphor. A particular motif, or metaphor, stands out for me: *water*. In the early traditions of both East and West, death entails a crossing over a river, usually facilitated by a ferryman.[8] Dante retells this story, in a Christian context, in his *Inferno*. And Tennyson makes the sea his central image in his famous poems on death, "Ulysses" and "Crossing the Bar" (as well as "Idylls of the King"). Accessible and traditional these poems may be, but who can forget that image: the aged Ulysses at the oars, heading out on the open sea, his back to the approaching unknown, the as-yet undisclosed. He hopes, in the end, to be united in death with his long-dead comrades-in-arms, including Achilles. He *hopes*. And with his last strength, he *strives*, even though the only certainty, the only thing he can actually *see*, as he sets out upon the vast ocean, is the receding shoreline of the real world, the world he must now leave. The sun sets, and as night falls, "the lights begin to twinkle from the rocks."

Homer's Ulysses–Odysseus—sails upon "the wine-dark sea."[9] I've been amused by some of the silly attempts by online commentators to explain how it could be that the sea was wine-colored. The symbolisms here should be obvious. The sea is dark:

it's mysterious, unfathomable, as is life and death—and also our subconscious. It is life-sustaining and useful (for instance, as a medium of travel or as a source of fish and whale-oil), but at the same time deeply perilous and life-threatening. And it's wine-colored: in reality it may be blue or blue-green or grey, but as a symbol of mystery and of the subconscious it is Dionysian, nonrational—and Dionysius was, of course, the god of wine. The juxtaposition of sea and sky is a powerful reminder of our twofold nature: We are Apollonian (the sky and sun above being the realm of Apollo), and we are Dionysian. We are rational and nonrational, conscious and subconscious, immanent and transcendent, mortal, yet aware (unlike the rest of nature) of our brief temporal existence within the incomprehensible vastness of eternity. We live on Ulysses' little boat between these poles.

My own experience, with regard to my dreams, is that water—in particular, water that flows, as in a stream—is a marker for sex or for erotic feeling. This would seem to contrast with the myth of a river separating life and death. Are there similarities between death and sex? In the throes of sex we may tend to lose our separate self. And Freud saw death (Thanatos) and sex (Eros) as the great duality of human life. In any case, rivers are a link: like roads, they lead us away from where we are, out to the encounter with the Other. But unlike roads, which lead from one terrestrial place to another, rivers lead inexorably to the sea. The sea is life, the scene of life's first beginning; and the sea is death, swallowing us up in its unfathomable vastness and depth—"this appalling ocean," says Melville, that surrounds our "insular Tahiti."[10]

Would we really want to live forever? It's true that we don't relish the prospect of leaving this life, this world, the people and things we love. But would everlasting life have any meaning? Values may be timeless, but *meaning* can be found—*encountered*—only in temporal existence, in the fleeting lived concrete of this world.

Chapter 6

Existence and Transcendence

Some four hundred years ago, Galileo made the revolutionary observation that the laws of the universe are to be found not in Holy Writ but in the laws of mathematics. With respect to objective reality, Galileo was right. Everything of which you and I and everyone else are able to have essentially the same experience can be measured and described mathematically. And the underpinnings of our *subjective* experience are also measurable and quantifiable. Our visual experience, for example, is dependent upon discrete rods and cones, and upon a certain number of nerve cells in certain brain areas, including, but not limited to, the visual cortex. The information that reaches those rods and cones are measurable, in terms of wavelength and frequency, as are the sounds that reach our ears. But how do we measure, quantitatively, our subjective, emotional experience of the color red or the sound of a Bach concerto or the beat and wail of jazz? How do we really measure the intensity of our pain, when the nurse asks us to give a number from one to ten? How do we give a quantitative description of our feeling of love for another human being, or for a work of art or element of nature that seems to address our deeper self?

There is a gap here—a gap that we explored in the "Hard Problem" of consciousness in Chapter 1, and my odometer, described at the beginning of Chapter 4, whose purpose was to surmount the quantifiable and visible here-and-now toward the unimaginable transcendent. Beyond the quantifiable and measurable lies mystery. In a real sense, both science and traditional religion, at least in its more ossified forms, reject true mystery. For science—or better, for scientism—mystery is merely whatever science has not yet solved. For traditional religion, mystery may be that which is beyond our power to know, but nothing is beyond God's power to know. And if the mystic finds unity with God, does he/she then know all that can be known? Unlikely, to say the least. I believe in true mystery. True mystery is beyond all possible explanation—or at least, our ability to truly imagine and explain. As Rudolf Otto said, "The truly 'mysterious' object is beyond our apprehension, not only because our knowledge has certain irremovable limits, but because in it we come upon something inherently 'wholly other' ..."[1]

True religious experience begins with mystical experience. Traditionally, that has been seen as a direct, unmediated experience of relation or unity with the transcendent/divine. Probably all religions that have endured have had their origin in an individual's religious experience—what Buber called an originating relational event, or what William James (*The Varieties of Religious Experience*) characterized as an experience of ineffability, such that "no adequate report of its contents can be given in words."[2] Like Moses at the Burning Bush, the mystic encounters (metaphorically, perhaps) Him who calls Himself "I Am That I Am."

Evelyn Underhill's book *Mysticism: A Study in the Nature and Development of Man's Spiritual Consciousness*, published in 1911 and revised in 1930, provides an overview of key aspects of religious mysticism. Though not a work of academic scholarship, this book provides something of an inside view, inasmuch as its author personally resonates, to a considerable degree, with the experiences reported by mystics through the ages, including those of the East but more especially those of the Christian tradition. An essential difference between Underhill's outlook and my own is evident in her earliest pages, where she declares herself explicitly to be a supernaturalist. The Absolute, with whom the mystics seek unity, is not in or of nature but above it—that is, it (or He) transcends it. As I've already indicated, I am not a supernaturalist and I am not in accord with the notion of unity with the Absolute, assuming that concept to mean that the self dissolves into some sort of cosmic unity, whether that unity involves a supernatural god or a secular transcendence or simply "the All." But I believe in the human orientation toward transcendence. And I found much in Underhill's book to applaud.

As to what mysticism is *not*, Underhill makes two emphatic points: First, mysticism is not to be confused with magic, with occult notions, with astrology or numerology, etc. Prefiguring Joseph Campbell's observations on ritual and John Potts' (*A History of Charisma*) references to St. Paul's letters to the Corinthians, Underhill notes that mysticism is not about trying to get some divine (magical) favor for oneself. This point leads into the second point: Mysticism, contrary to common perception, is not quietism. Although the mystic may undergo a period of contemplation and even withdrawal from all worldly affairs, the mystical experience leads ultimately not to quietistic withdrawal but to a renewed, active engagement with the world—a heightened, loving appreciation for the world and all that dwell therein.

Underhill sounds core existentialist themes: "This revealed Reality is apprehended by way of participation, not by way of observation."[3] And, prefiguring the language of Sartre: "[T]he person emerges from a smaller limited world of existence into a larger world of being."[4]

Like Campbell, Jung, John Dominic Crossan, and others, Underhill recognizes that the ineffable quality of mystical experience requires connotative rather than denotative (literal) expression if it is to be communicated to others. "All kinds of symbolic language come naturally to the articulate mystic... so naturally that he sometimes forgets to explain that his utterance is but symbolic—a desperate attempt to translate the truth of that world into the beauty of this. It is here that mysticism joins hands with music and poetry." And: "The mystic, as a rule, cannot do without symbol and image, inadequate to his vision though they must always be: for his experience must be expressed if it is to be communicated, and its actuality is inexpressible except in some sidelong way, some hint or parallel which will stimulate the dormant intuition of the reader and convey, as all poetic language does, something beyond its surface sense."[5]

Although Underhill, as a believing Christian, accepts the doctrine of the Trinity, she sees — as any of us, regardless of our belief or unbelief, can see — the symbolism of that doctrine. The Father represents absolute transcendence, the indescribable, inaccessible "I am that I am," the extremity of our imagination. The Son is the visible and accessible "Word made flesh," Son of God and Son of Man. The Holy Spirit is the indwelling divine spark, or inner light (to use terms familiar to Quakers) that Jesus promised at the Last Supper as he took leave of his disciples. The Son's life on this earth is temporal; the Father is eternal and transcendent, and thus, essentially inaccessible to us; but the Holy Spirit, as described (according to Scripture) by Jesus, is both transcendent and immanent; immortal, yet indwelling in each of us mortal human beings. Even for those of us who reject supernatural literalism, this allegory speaks powerfully to our nature as sentient beings with a consciousness, and a will, that transcends the immanently given and the selfishly imperative.

This leads Underhill to a key observation: mysticism, and religion in general, has a dual aspect of immanence and transcendence. And although religious experience, for some people, tends more toward the immanent or indwelling and for others more toward the transcendent, that dual aspect is inescapable. In the religious — and mystical — experience, the Absolute, the "wholly other," whether immanent or transcendent, is somehow to be encountered and joined with.

Religion scholar Ann Taves[6] notes the difference between the Lutheran and early Catholic doctrine of the Eucharist and, on the other hand, that of the Catholic Church since the Fourth Lateran Council of 1215. In the former concept, the wine and wafer do not become the blood and body of Christ until received (ingested) by the believer. Here, the joining of believer and the Absolute has a quality of immanence. But in the latter concept, the wine and wafer become the blood and body of Christ, prior to the believer's reception, through the actions of the sacerdotal priest at the altar when he performs the grandiose rite of the Elevation of the Blessed Sacrament and intones Christ's (Latinized[7]) words *Hoc est corpus meum* (This is my body). And, as Taves points out, this adoption of a transcendental approach to the Eucharist roughly coincided with the building of the ornately grandiose Gothic cathedrals with their pointed arches, pointing toward transcendent Heaven.

Quaker (Religious Society of Friends) worship and religious architecture is at the opposite pole from that of Roman Catholicism, particularly of the period from the high Middle Ages to the Second Vatican Council of the 1960s. The Quaker meetinghouse is plain and unadorned, lacking iconography— even the Cross—and the paraphernalia of ritual. There is no leader and no liturgy. The congregation sits in silence until one or another, moved by "the Spirit," rises and speaks. From their first gatherings in seventeenth-century England, Quakers (Friends) spoke of the "indwelling Christ." Thus, Quakerism has always been at the "immanent" end of the spectrum. As one who was raised in this tradition, I can appreciate this sense of immanence and equality, as well as the lack of authoritarianism and elaborate dogma. Yet I can't help but ask: Might there be something missing?

Like many Catholics who have left the Church—and, in some cases, have left supernaturalism altogether—Joseph Campbell understood well the appeal and power of exalted ritual, which expresses our human longing toward transcendence. And so do I, although never having lived with it, I am better able to live without it. I feel rather homeless in this regard: dissatisfied with a religion (Quakerism) that seems to lack a full sense of transcendence and duality (whether duality is to be overcome or to be incorporated into one's spiritual life), yet unable to participate wholeheartedly in rituals that I regard as purely symbolic. But despite my lack of doctrinal belief and liturgical participation, I take comfort in the existence of both the immanent simplicity of Quaker worship and the majesty of the great churches and cathedrals and the exalted rituals, iconography, and music of the "transcendent" traditions. The very existence of these contrasting but vital aspects of the human spirit brings a sense of connectedness with that shared spirit. To imagine the absence of these traditions — immanent and transcendent—is to imagine a bleak spiritual desert.

I have been accused, perhaps justifiably, of being overly intellectual in my approach to "spiritual" matters. In his classic *The Varieties of Religious Experience*, William James addresses the dilemma: "I do believe that feeling is the deeper source of religion, and that philosophies and theological formulas are secondary products. ..." But James continues: "We are thinking beings, and we cannot exclude the intellect from participating in any of our functions. Even in soliloquizing with ourselves, we construe our feelings intellectually. ... Moreover, we must exchange our feelings with one another, and in doing so we have to speak, and to use general and abstract verbal formulas. Conceptions and constructions are thus a necessary part of our religion. ..."[8]

But then again, as Rudolf Otto points out, when we try to preserve or communicate our experience of the numinous, the inescapable process of description and objectification that this entails causes the numinous quality of the experience to fade. Can ritual, as a symbolic re-enactment of the numinous experience, recapture or induce that experience in its original power? No. Can it serve as a helpful reminder and a comforting reassurance? Perhaps. More likely for some than for others.

The sense of duality in religion—self and non-self, immanence and transcendence—can be found (although I have to say that it took some effort on my part to find it) in the Quaker mystic Rufus Jones (1863-1948). Although I have much the same quarrel with supernaturalism in Jones's writings as I do with earlier mystics, I was impressed by this pertinent and well-stated bit of wisdom: "The consciousness of 'self' and the consciousness of 'other' are born together, and we cannot use one of them as the searchlight to find the other. There comes a leap of 'acknowledgment' of other persons, which is of a very different order from our attainment of the sense of the reality of external objects."[9] I'm reminded here of my little helicopters, mentioned at the opening of Chapter 1: I was aware, *simultaneously*, of my being inside my helicopter and other people inside theirs. Although Jones, in keeping with the tradition of religious mysticism, goes on to say that in that same instant we become aware of "the divine Self," I would say that we become aware that we live in a shared and boundless world that draws us toward transcendence.

Evelyn Underhill does not propose that we all should, or can, become mystics of the stature of St. John of the Cross, St. Catherine of Siena, St. Teresa of Ávila, or Meister Eckhart—or her contemporary, Rufus Jones (whom she mentions). But she does propose that we "meet them half way," and she makes this suggestion:

> Willfully yet tranquilly refuse the messages which countless other aspects of the world of objects are sending and concentrate your whole attention on the act of loving sight. . . . First, you will perceive about you a strange and deepening quietness, a slowing down of our feverish mental time.

Next, you will become aware of a heightened significance, an intensified existence in the thing at which you look. As you, with all your consciousness, lean out towards it, an answering current will meet yours. It seems as though the barrier between its life and your own, between subject and object, had melted away.[10]

Although I have critiqued the monist assumptions of Krishnamurti and Watts, this passage brings to mind their intense experience of nature undiluted by extraneous and self-centered concerns. It reminds us of Buber also. "I consider a tree," he says, and proceeds to list the many ways that we might do so, looking upon the tree as *it*. "It can, however, also come about, if I have both will and grace, that in considering the tree I become bound up in relation to it. The tree is now no longer *It*. I have been seized by the power of exclusiveness."[11] I have encountered the tree as *Thou*, and in every such encounter my own being is disclosed, for "There is no *I* taken in itself, but only the *I* of the primary word *I-Thou*. ..."[12]

These quotations from Evelyn Underhill and Martin Buber contain key terms and concepts that are central to our entire discussion. Describing the relational event—whether with a tree, a flower, the sea, the Grand Canyon, or a fellow human being—Underhill speaks of a sense of "heightened significance" and "an intensified existence." And Buber speaks of being "seized by the power of exclusiveness." In contrast to the meaningless, amorphous ooze of raw existence that nauseates Roquentin in Sartre's novel, the relational event—the meeting of I and Thou—discloses the *particularity* of the Other and of ourselves. This particularity is not the "uniqueness" of comparative difference or objective individuality, nor is the Other merely a generic fellow human or sentient being with whom we can empathize, important though empathy assuredly is. Rather, the Other is disclosed as absolute and *wholly other* (in Rudolf Otto's sense).

Like the God of Moses and the divine Absolute of the mystics, both we ourselves and the Other can say, "I am that I am." In relation and disclosure lies mystery: the mystery of particularity, of transcendence, of *being*. Hence, for me, the futility of seeking to dissolve the self in the Other or in the Absolute. It is in the *mysterium* of encounter and relation—*meeting*—that we realize our humanity, and that our life takes on meaning.

The mystics have often told of their passage through the dark night of despair on their perilous spiritual journey—a despair at being unable to speak the primary word *I-Thou*. Those of us who have suffered serious depression have also known dark nights. In such a state, there is a desperately sad realization that death can provide no real escape, as Sartre's Roquentin (*Nausea*) realizes: "I thought vaguely of doing away with myself... but my death would have been superfluous as well. .... I was superfluous for all eternity."[13] To live is to exist, but to die (whether by one's own hand or otherwise) is not simply to *not* exist: it is, rather, to *cease to exist*, to be erased. Life and death alike are wrapped in the despair at not being able to really *be*, to make the transition from superfluous, contingent existence to *being*. Death brings an end to suffering, but it also definitively brings an end to any hope of *being*, that longed-for Eden of the soul. The *person* will die; the *personage* will be forever unrealized. Had I not been born, there would be no problem, no existent longing impossibly for *being*, "longing for light," said Job, "and finding none." In this state, like Job, we curse the day we were born. I recall that in that state I saw even the high and mighty as similarly hopeless and superfluous: "High and low are there alike."[14]

What is this elusive, longed-for *being*? I turn again to Roquentin (*Nausea*), sitting with his beer in a bistro as a jazz song plays on the jukebox. Up to this point in the novel, Roquentin has been experiencing a profound sense of the futility of existence. Things, and even people—himself included—simply *exist*. To exist is simply to *be there*, to be superfluous (*de trop*), to be subject to measurement and comparison, to be gripped in the fate, as Paul Tillich (*The Courage to Be*) described, of being "contingent in every respect, of having no ultimate necessity."[15] But then the music begins. Roquentin hears the sounds of the singer and the instruments; he hears, too, the scratching and occasional skipping of the old, well-worn record. He realizes, in that moment, that he is in the presence of *being*. "[I]f I were to get up and rip this record from the [turn]table..., if I were to break it in two, I wouldn't reach *it*. It is beyond—always beyond... It does not exist because it has nothing superfluous. ... It *is*. And I, too, wanted to *be*."[16]

We saw earlier how apt the musical analogy is. Some music seems contrived and superfluous; the composer's struggle to come up with something is all too obvious. Successful music, however, seems somehow to transcend deliberate human effort; we know that in actual fact works of creativity do not happen without human effort, but when a song, a painting, or a poem is successful as a work of art, we say that it seems inspired. A religious metaphor comes to mind: *And the Word became flesh and dwelt among us, full of grace and truth*. There is an ineffable, numinous aspect here; we're not quite sure why we're moved— changed, even—by good and great music and art. In a rather similar way, we are affected by the "charisma" of certain men and women, a quality that seems larger than the sum of their describable characteristics. The people who affect us most profoundly and lastingly tend to be people in whom character and action are infused with a sense of authenticity. Like great music and art, they seem to transcend commonplace existence. They are not *de trop*; they are irreplaceable.

As Pascal said, I am not a necessary being; there is no reason or explanation for my existence as just this subjective consciousness. I am not "a part of God's plan." There is no god, and there is no plan. If I am to be necessary in any way, I need to *make* myself necessary in the world. Certainly the world will survive without me. But just as great art, music, and literature make us more whole, so too can the individual find ways to make the world—our fellow humans—more whole, whether on a cultural, physical, or personal level.

Being is numinous, existence is not. This is not to say that existence is bad; existence is simply that which exists. And this is not to say that *being* is supernatural. There is only one nature, one reality, and we are in it; we are a part of it. But to be human is to have a consciousness that transcends the immediately given, an imagination that transcends what exists, and that is unsatisfied—indeed, cannot fully live—on the plane of mere existence. The scope of our consciousness, and the mystery and ineffability of our condition, sets up a creative tension and impels us toward creativity and transcendence. *Being* points beyond the determinism of our material existence and the incidental character of our subjective selfhood. It points toward relation.

True mystery is numinous. Mere "mysterianism" simply means that we don't know. True mystery is the *mysterium fascinans* and the *mysterium tremendum*—the "wholly other" toward whom we reach, out of our own whole otherness, in the hope not of perfect unity but of meeting and meaning. Such meeting is fated to be forever incomplete. It is, thus, a mystical experience.

As the mystics have taught us, as have also the existentialists, we cannot dwell on airy, mystic heights. Our life is in the world, a world that calls us to relation, to participation, to action. As Unamuno taught us, we must make ourselves irreplaceable, finding and doing that which we are uniquely equipped and called to do. As Ortega y Gasset told us, we are thus able to be a *personage*, not necessarily rich in fame, but possibly rich in *being*. As St. Teresa knew, both Mary and Martha are needed: our bodies need sustenance and our souls need confirmation.

Martin Buber said that he lived on "the narrow ridge." There are many possible interpretations of that statement (in addition to his own[17]); for me, perhaps the most powerful interpretation of that image is this: As I said at the beginning, there is no reason why I find myself here, in this body, in this time and place. Thus, I find myself on the narrow ridge between grace and absurdity. The fact that I am me is gratuitous, and this fact is, for me, both fortuitous—pregnant with the gift of existence and the possibility of *being*—and meaningless, in the sense that there is no cause or purpose behind the fact. The ridge is indeed narrow. We can look to one side and see grace and redemption, but on the other side yawns the abyss. Can we not simply drop off the ridge into the cooling waters of grace and redemption and find there our lasting home? Many would say "yes." I would say: Keep walking! The narrow ridge leads, as Buber tells us, to that which is as yet undisclosed; to encounter and relation, and to responsibility. And if, as Buber suggested, I have both will and grace, I may come to know what it is to *be*.

The importance of Rufus Jones's insight—the simultaneous realization of self and other—cannot be overstated. It gives natural and powerful support to what would otherwise be a moralistic injunction: Love thy neighbor as thyself. Without the neighbor, there is no self. Mere sentience does not create a self—only the presence of the Other can do that. Together with Pascal's experience, quoted at the outset, this insight helps to tie together the ideas of this book. We have explored the mysteries of consciousness and seen the apparent inability of science to solve them. We have seen how art, myth, and religion would have emerged as human consciousness reached the level of transcendent awareness, as explained by Raymond Tallis and others. The neurologist (Tallis) confirms the religionist (Jones) in this respect: With the emergence of self-awareness and the awareness of other selves come the awareness of the beyond, the transcendent. And although Jones saw the transcendent as supernatural and divine, it need not be so, as Tallis and others aver.

This drive toward relation and transcendence is not the same as the drive, evolved through natural selection and adaptation, to cooperate with others, to engage in reciprocity, to form communities, to care for one's children. It is a drive born of the nature of human consciousness. It is a drive born of the human need for meaning. And although this drive can never be truly and fully satisfied, we may well find a measure of meaning and fulfillment on the way.

Subjective consciousness either involves absolute mystery or absolute determinism. If the latter, there is no "wholly other" and no true I-Thou relation. We are in Sartre's (Roquentin's) city park, experiencing the nausea of viscous existence. In this viscous world of absolute determinism, we are (each of us) necessary only in the sense that reality could not have been otherwise. But that is not our condition. If we are to be necessary, we must make ourselves so. If we are to find meaning, we must go forth and find it in authentic *meeting*. Like the mystics returning from the mountaintop to the world of men and women, like Moses returning to his people after encountering I Am That I Am, we mortal existents return from the experience of mystery to our existing world with a fresh appreciation of *being*—mine, thine, and ours.

Endnotes

Chapter 1

1. Pascal, p. 48. Also quoted in Friedman, *Worlds of Existentialism*, p. 39.

2. Quoted in Humphrey, pp. 155-56.

3. See Holt, pp. 263-65.

4. In Douglas R. Hofstadter and Daniel C. Dennett, *The Mind's I: Fantasies and Reflections on Self and Soul* (New York: Basic Books, 1981), p. 47. For another of the few writings on this mystery, see the article by Tim S. Roberts, "The Even Harder Problem of Consciousness," listed in the bibliography.

5. PhilArchive, Centre for Digital Philosophy, University of Western Ontario, 2015 (Philpapers.org/rec/KLAWAI-3).

6. Pascal, p. 67. Also quoted in Friedman, *Worlds of Existentialism*, p. 41.

7. Nagel, pp. 68-69.

8. For Kant, we humans are noumenal because we are free, and we're free because we're rational and thus not totally bound by material needs and concerns. I'm aware that in my own use of the words "noumenon" and "noumenal" here and elsewhere in this book, I'm taking some liberties of interpretation, but without, I hope, abandoning the essential meaning.

9. Tallis, *Seeing Ourselves*, pp. 233ff. Libet's findings have also been critiqued on more technical grounds in the light of subsequent research; see, e.g., Seth, pp. 220-24. See also Dennett, pp. 154-67, for intensive discussion of Libet.

10. Interview with Robert Lawrence Kuhn, closertotruth.com/topics/consciousness.

11. Dehaene, p. 264.

12. Anil Seth (*Being You*) covers this well in his chapter on free will. I particularly like his quote from Schopenhauer: "Man

can *do* what he wills, but he cannot *will* what he wills [my emphases]." (See p. 225.)

13. Gelernter, pp. 171-72.

14. Equally puzzling is the fact that it was Humphrey, in that same book (*Soul Dust*), who furnished the Michel Bitbol quote which I cited earlier. If Humphrey recognizes the mystery of subjective identity, how can he not recognize the mystery of the "Hard Problem"? Douglas Hofstadter seems similarly inconsistent.

Richard Dawkins says this about Humphrey's social adaptiveness theory of consciousness: "I find Humphrey's reasoning persuasive . . . [but] I am not sure that this helps us to understand consciousness." (Richard Dawkins, *The Selfish Gene* [second edition, Oxford University Press, 1989], p. 281.)

15. Pascal, p. 94. Also quoted in Friedman, *Worlds of Existentialism*, p. 39.

16. *Saturday* (New York: Doubleday, 2005), p. 262.

17. Dennett, p. 455.

18. Hofstadter and Dennett, *The Mind's I*, p. 8.

19. See Dennett, p. 455.

20. See Searle, pp. 20-23.

21. The problem with any notion that subjective feelings can be measured is illustrated by this common experience: you go to the hospital, and the nurse asks, "On a scale of one to ten, how severe is your pain?" It has been said that the correct answer is always "eight"; if you say "nine" or "ten," they won't believe you, and if you give a number less than eight, they won't give you the good stuff.

22. Sacks, *The River of Consciousness*, p. 173.

23. *Washington Post* online, July 26, 2019.

24. Solms, p. 266.

25. Edelman, p. 152. See also Gerald M. Edelman, Joseph A. Gally, and Bernard J. Baars, "Biology of Consciousness," *Frontiers in Psychology*, 25 January 2011.

26. Solms, p. 301.
27. Edelman, p. 3.
28. Seth, p. 56.
29. Graziano, p. 144.
30. Graziano, p. 39.
31. Penrose is also well-known for proposing a quantum-mechanics theory of consciousness. See Dehaene, pp. 263-64, for a brief rebuttal.
32. Solms, p. 273.
33. Thomas Metzinger, *The Ego Tunnel: The Science of the Mind and the Myth of the Self* (New York: Basic Books, 2009).
34. Philip A. Goff, *Galileo's Error: Foundations for a New Science of Consciousness* (New York: Pantheon, 2019).
35. Bernardo Kastrup, *The Idea of the World: A multi-disciplinary argument for the mental nature of reality* (London: iff Books, 2019). See a brief discussion of Kastrup in Meghan O'Gieblyn, *God Human Animal Machine: Technology, Metaphor, and the Search for Meaning* (New York: Doubleday, 2021), pp. 181-85.
36. www.samharris.org/blog/the-mystery-of-consciousness.
37. Annaka Harris, *Conscious: A Brief Guide to the Fundamental Mystery of the Mind* (New York: Harper, 2019), p. 71.
38. Bruce Hood, *The Self Illusion: How the Social Brain Creates Identity* (Oxford University Press, 2012).
39. I will revisit the "self" debate in a later chapter.
40. Solms, p. 208.
41. Maritain, *Existence and the Existent*, quoted in Friedman, *Worlds of Existentialism*, p. 353.

Chapter 2

1. A highly informative and interesting book, with which I am largely in agreement, except for the authors' supernaturalist conclusions.
2. Newberg et al., pp. 46-47.

3. Newberg et al., p. 63.

4. Feinberg and Mallatt (*Consciousness Demystified*) place the rudimentary origins of consciousness in the Cambrian period, about a half a billion years ago, when simple neural reflex arcs began to expand into much more complex circuits, a development accompanied by the evolution of more proficient sensory organs.

5. Well, perhaps not quite as suddenly as that! The time frame is a matter of dispute.

6. Tallis, *Michelangelo's Finger*, p. 59.

7. *Michelangelo's Finger*, p. 119.

8. *Michelangelo's Finger*, p. 143.

9. Edward O. Wilson, *Consilience: The Unity of Knowledge* (New York: Vintage Books, 1998), p. 254.

10. Freud, pp. 10-11.

11. Eiseley, p. 144.

12. Fromm, pp. 7-8.

13. Hart, p. 2.

14. Eiseley, p. 136.

15. Fromm, p. 51.

16. Buber, p. 11.

17. Matthews, pp. 34-35.

Chapter 3

1. Robinson Jeffers eloquently disagreed with the view that I'm expressing. "The beauty of things was born before eyes and sufficient to itself; the heart-breaking beauty / Will remain when there is no heart to break for it." (From "Credo," in *The Collected Poetry of Robinson Jeffers*. Ed. Tim Hunt. Stanford University Press, 1988-2001.) Quoted in Hart, p. 54.

2. Otto, p. 26.

3. Otto, p. 68.

4. I've had the wonderful experience of visiting the Clyfford Still Museum in Denver. Although many of his paintings

have areas of bare canvas, others seem, at a distance, to be thoroughly covered in paint, with rich and variegated color and texture and his signature verticalities, which Still himself characterized as representative of the human need to stand upright against raw existence. But on close inspection of these often monumental paintings, tiny spots of bare canvas can be seen scattered throughout the painting. Raw existence—and non-existence—is always there, behind our human projects, our assertive creativity, and our search for meaning.

5. Otto, p. 70.

6. Dutton, p. 2.

7. Dutton, p. 110.

8. Dutton, p. 54.

9. Levitin works the sexual selection theme rather hard, going so far as to mention that major rock stars have no shortage of women throwing themselves at them. But the same can be said of famous athletes as well as famous (and good-looking) killers (Ted Bundy, Robert Chambers, Scott Peterson, or even Joran van der Sloot).

10. Ball, p. 246.

11. Ball, p. 241.

12. Quoted in Ball, p. 30.

13. *Pace* Levitin, the jury is still out as to whether music was a precursor to language. The famous neurologist Oliver Sacks (*Musicophilia*, p. 242) asks, "Did speech... precede music (as Steven Pinker suggests); did song precede speech (as Darwin thought); or did both develop simultaneously (as Mithen proposes)?" I lean toward Mithen, but, as I said, the jury is still out.

14. Ball, p. 402.

15. Quoted in Ball, p. 383.

16. *Reductionism in Art and Brain Science.* Kandel's use of the word "reductionism" is potentially confusing, even

with his attempt to clarify: "[A]lthough the reductionist approaches of scientists and artists are not identical in their aims... they are analogous" (p. 6).

17. Calvin, p. 93.
18. Sacks, *Musicophilia*, p. 241.
19. Quoted in Sacks, *Musicophilia*, p. 213.
20. See, generally, *Michelangelo's Finger*, particularly pp. 142-43.
21. Tallis, *Summers of Discontent*, p. 47.
22. Buber, p. 10.
23. Read, p. 75.

Chapter 4

1. Some writers have asserted that the ascription of conscious intention and agency to animals and things was adaptive for our early ancestors and was the source of religious belief— see, e.g. Pascal Boyer, *Religion Explained: The Evolutionary Origins of Religious Thought* (New York: Basic Books, 2001).
2. Armstrong, p. 16.
3. Jung et al., *Man and His Symbols*, p. 95.
4. Eliade, p. 122.
5. Armstrong, p. 17.
6. Cassirer, p. 19.
7. Exodus 3:14. In some Bibles, including my family's German Bible (based on Luther's translation), as well as in some English translations, God says, "I will be what I will be" (*Ich werde sein, der ich sein werde*). Perhaps there's an "existentialist" theme here: open possibility rather than closed reality. But most versions I've looked at, whether Protestant, Catholic (Douay-Rheims), or Hebrew (in English translation), have "I am that [or 'who' or 'what'] I am."
8. John 1:14.
9. Mark 14:22-23.

10. Donald J. Moore, *Martin Buber: Prophet of Religious Secularism* (New York: Fordham University Press, 1996), p. xxi.

11. Matthew 26:6-13; Mark 14:5-9. Someone once asked me, "But how do you know that that actually happened? How do you know that the story is true?" It should be obvious that historicity is not the point here, or with any of the other Biblical passages that I cite. This is about *meaning*, not history.

12. Jesus' praise of Mary should not be taken as a diminution of Martha's contribution as cook. As St. Teresa of Ávila said, "To give our Lord a perfect hospitality, Mary and Martha must combine."

13. My quotations from this show may not be precise but are as close as I can recall.

14. He had, of course, been king, but abdicated before he could be crowned. Thus—fittingly, given what the War years revealed of his shortage of character and patriotism—he was never anointed.

15. Potts, p. 221.

16. José Ortega y Gasset, *In Search of Goethe from Within*, quoted in Friedman, *Worlds of Existentialism*, p. 121.

17. Sartre, p. 174. The translator (Lloyd Alexander) of this particular edition of *Nausea* renders *"de trop"* as "in the way," which perhaps doesn't quite capture the sense of being superfluous, i.e., a needless addition to meaningless existence.

18. Sartre, p. 175.

19. This word is more commonly used in scientific contexts, notably biology, chemistry, and mathematics. But the underlying idea is of similarity of form or structure. In Eliade's usage, the form of a thing remains the same, but its meaning, for the human experiencer, diverges.

20. Sartre, p. 176.

21. W. B. Yeats, "The Circus Animals' Desertion."
22. Jung, *Modern Man in Search of a Soul*, p. 65.
23. Quoted in Smith, p. 33.
24. Cf. St. Paul, who recognized that individuals have varied spiritual gifts to offer the community (I Corinthians 12:4-6).
25. Quoted in Smith, p. 240.
26. Campbell, *Thou Art That*, p. 11.
27. Watts, p. 86.
28. Watts, p. 110.
29. Krishnamurti, p. 86.
30. Blackmore, p. 167.
31. Krishnamurti, *Freedom from the Known* (New York: Harper & Row, 1969), p. 22.
32. Buber drew a distinction between experience and relation: "As experience, the world belongs to the primary word *I-It*. The primary word *I-Thou* establishes the world of relation." (*I and Thou*, p. 6.) Thus, rather than speaking of a numinous experience, Buber might have preferred to speak of a numinous relational event, or a numinous meeting.
33. The moment of experience has to have some temporal extension in order to be "digested"; it cannot be the unextended instant between past and future.
34. Tallis, *Seeing Ourselves*, p. 179.
35. "Time Travelers." *New York Times Magazine*, November 18, 2018.
36. Newberg et al., p. 85.
37. Armstrong, p. 19.
38. Surely this ceremony also celebrates the persistence of an ancient, proud, but marginalized indigenous culture in the face of an invasive dominant culture.
39. See Moore, p. 159.
40. Armstrong, p. 107.
41. Tallis, *Seeing Ourselves*, p. 15.

Chapter 5

1. Tallis, *Seeing Ourselves*, p. 363.
2. One might think that progeny would be one of the surer consolations; after all, there are only two basic instincts in all of life: survival and reproduction. Progeny—offspring—carry on our genes—our biology—and their nurture and upbringing is perhaps the most momentous project of our lives. Normally the bonds in this relationship are strong indeed. But in the end, however much we love them, they are not us. As Tennyson's Ulysses says, after expressing his love and pride toward his son, Telemachus: "He works his work, I mine."
3. Nagel, p. 243.
4. Unamuno, p. 269.
5. I recall reading of a young American soldier or Marine, mortally wounded at Okinawa, who calmly reassured his comrades: "It won't be long now."
6. Chelsea, VT: Chelsea Green Publishing Company, 1992, p. 101. Prior to her long marriage to Scott Nearing, which is thoroughly explored in this book, Helen (*née* Knothe) had a close relationship with Krishnamurti. In an early chapter of the book, Helen reveals her feelings toward—and candid assessment of—this rather complex man.
7. By "nothingness" Malraux no doubt had in mind both death and absurdity, or "thrownness."
8. See, of course, Hermann Hesse's *Siddhartha*.
9. Regrettably, not all of the many translations of *The Odyssey* use this term. I've been reading Samuel Butler's translation, for instance, and to my great disappointment Butler never refers to the wine-dark sea (simply "the sea"). But the term does occur in many of the other translations, as well it should: the original Greek has οἴνοψ: wine.
10. *Moby Dick* (New York: Rinehart, 1948), p. 273; quoted in Friedman, *Worlds of Existentialism*, p. 60. Although I have,

here, interpreted Melville's words as a metaphor for death, the full passage suggests an existentialist theme as well as the observations of Erich Fromm, quoted earlier. Here is Melville's passage: "As this appalling ocean surrounds the verdant land, so in the soul of man there lies one insular Tahiti, full of peace and joy, but encompassed by all the horrors of the half-known life. ... Push not off from that isle, thou canst never return!"

Chapter 6

1. Otto, p. 28.
2. James, p. 380.
3. Underhill, p. 333.
4. E. D. Starbuck, *The Psychology of Religion: An Empirical Study of the Growth of Religious Consciousness* (London: Walter Scott, 1899), quoted in Underhill, p. 177.
5. Underhill, pp. 79-80.
6. Ann Taves, *Religious Experience Reconsidered: A Building-Block Approach to the Study of Religion and Other Special Things* (Princeton University Press, 2009), pp. 158ff.
7. The Latin (as opposed to vernacular) Mass is, of course, integral to placing the sacrament on a transcendental plane, clothed in glamour and mystery, above mundane reality, thus enhancing the believer's desire for union with the Highest.
8. James, pp. 431-32.
9. Rufus M. Jones, *New Eyes for Invisibles* (New York: Macmillan, 1944), p. 151.
10. Underhill, p. 301.
11. Buber, p. 7.
12. Buber, p. 4.
13. Sartre, pp. 128-29.
14. Job 3:3, 4, 19.
15. Tillich, p. 44.

16. Sartre, p. 175.

17. "I have occasionally described my standpoint to my friends as the 'narrow ridge.' I wanted by this to express that I did not rest on the broad upland of a system that includes a series of sure statements about the absolute, but on a narrow rocky ridge between the gulfs where there is not sureness of expressible knowledge but the certainty of meeting what remains undisclosed." (Martin Buber, *Between Man and Man*, trans. by Ronald Gregor Smith. London: Kegan Paul, 1974, p. 184.) Maurice Friedman (*Martin Buber: The Life of Dialogue*) gives us permission, in effect, to add our own interpretations of this beautiful metaphor.

A Slightly Annotated Bibliography

Armstrong, Karen. *A Short History of Myth*. Edinburgh: Canongate, 2005.

Ball, Philip. *The Music Instinct: How Music Works and Why We Can't Do Without It*. Oxford University Press, 2010.

Blackmore, Susan. *Consciousness*. New York and London: Sterling, 2005.

Buber, Martin. *I and Thou*. Trans. by Ronald Gregor Smith. New York: Charles Scribner's Sons, 1937. For more on Buber, see Friedman's two books, infra. Another source of insight into Buber's thought is Donald J. Moore, *Martin Buber: Prophet of Religious Secularism*. New York: Fordham University Press, 1996.

Calvin, William H. *A Brief History of the Mind: From Apes to Intellect and Beyond*. Oxford University Press, 2004.

Campbell, Joseph. *The Hero with a Thousand Faces*. New York: MJF Books, 1949.

_____. *Thou Art That: Transforming Religious Metaphor*. Novato, CA: New World Library, 2001.

Cassirer, Ernst. *Language and Myth*. Trans. by Susanne K. Langer. New York: Dover, 1953.

Chalmers, David J. *The Conscious Mind: In Search of a Fundamental Theory*. Oxford University Press, 1996.

Crossan, John Dominic. *The Dark Interval: Toward a Theology of Story*. Niles, IL: Argus Communications, 1975.

_____. *Jesus: A Revolutionary Biography*. HarperSanFrancisco, 1995. I've read other books by Crossan—all of them rewarding—but I'm unable to recall their titles at present.

_____, William L. Craig, William F. Buckley, ed. Paul Copan. *Will the Real Jesus Please Stand Up?* Grand Rapids, MI: Baker Books, 1998.

Damasio, Antonio. *Descartes' Error: Emotion, Reason and the Human Brain*. Penguin Books, 1994.

_____. *Self Comes to Mind: Constructing the Conscious Brain*. New York: Vintage Books, 2010.

Dehaene, Stanislas. *Consciousness and the Brain: Deciphering How the Brain Codes Our Thoughts*. Penguin Books, 2014.

Dennett, Daniel. *Consciousness Explained*. New York and Boston: Little, Brown, 1991.

Dutton, Denis. *The Art Instinct: Beauty, Pleasure, and Human Evolution*. London and New York: Bloomsbury Press, 2009.

Edelman, Gerald M. *Wider Than the Sky: The Phenomenal Gift of Consciousness*. New Haven, CT: Yale University Press, 2004.

Eiseley, Loren. *The Unexpected Universe*. New York: Harcourt, Brace & World, 1969. Some of the disappointing political views of Eiseley, Campbell, and other writers whom I admire are difficult to ignore, but I will resist the temptation to write a retort. My present book is not intended as a vehicle for political debate or a return to the controversies of the 1960s.

Eliade, Mircea. *The Sacred and the Profane: The Nature of Belief*. Trans. by Willard R. Trask. New York: Harcourt, 1959.

Feinberg, Todd E. and Jon M. Mallatt. *Consciousness Demystified*. Cambridge, MA: MIT Press, 2018.

Flynn, Thomas. *Existentialism*. New York and London: Sterling, 2006.

Frankl, Viktor. *Man's Search for Meaning*. Trans. by Ilse Lasch. Boston: Beacon Press, 1959.

Freud, Sigmund. *Civilization and Its Discontents*. Trans. by James Strachey. New York and London: W.W. Norton, 2010. First published 1930.

Friedman, Maurice. *Martin Buber: The Life of Dialogue*. New York: Harper, 1955.

_____, ed. *Worlds of Existentialism: A Critical Reader*. New York: Random House, 1964. A number of my quotes from various authors can be found in excerpts from their works included in this book, including those by Pascal (*Pensées*), Maritain (*Existence and the Existent*), Ortega y Gasset (*In Search of Goethe from Within*), Frankl (*Man's Search for Meaning*), and Melville (*Moby Dick*). I had, of course, previously read these latter two books, but it was in Friedman's excerpts that these particular quotations jumped out at me.

Fromm, Erich. *The Art of Loving: An Inquiry into the Nature of Love*. New York: Harper Colophon, 1956.

Gelernter, David. *The Tides of Mind: Uncovering the Spectrum of Consciousness*. New York: Liveright, 2016.

Graziano, Michael. *Consciousness and the Social Brain*. Oxford University Press, 2013.

Hart, George. *Inventing the Language to Tell It: Robinson Jeffers and the Biology of Consciousness*. New York: Fordham University Press, 2013.

Holt, Jim. *Why Does the World Exist? An Existential Detective Story*. New York: Liveright, 2012.

Humphrey, Nicholas. *Soul Dust: The Magic of Consciousness*. Princeton University Press, 2011.

James, William. *The Varieties of Religious Experience*. New York: Longmans, Green, 1902. I have my grandfather's copy: nineteenth impression, 1910.

Jung, Carl G., et al. *Man and His Symbols*. New York: Doubleday, 1964.

_____. *Modern Man in Search of a Soul*. New York: Harcourt, 1933.

Kandel, Eric R. *Reductionism in Art and Brain Science: Bridging the Two Cultures*. New York: Columbia University Press, 2016.

Krishnamurti, J. *All the Marvelous Earth*. Ojai, CA: Krishnamurti Foundation of America, 2000. Brief excerpts from Krishnamurti's lectures and writings, each accompanied by a photograph of nature or, in some cases, of human activity. Various photographers.

Levitin, Daniel J. *This Is Your Brain on Music: The Science of a Human Obsession*. Dutton, 2006 (paperback 2016).

Lévy-Strauss, Claude. *Myth and Meaning: Cracking the Code of Culture*. University of Toronto Press, 1978 (paperback: New York: Schocken Books, 1979).

Matthews, Eric. *Merleau-Ponty: A Guide for the Perplexed*. London and New York: Continuum, 2006.

Mithen, Steven J. *The Prehistory of the Mind*. London and New York: Thames & Hudson, 1996.

Nagel, Thomas. *The View from Nowhere*. Oxford University Press, 1986.

Newberg, Andrew, Eugene D'Aquili, and Vince Rause. *Why God Won't Go Away: Brain Science and the Biology of Belief*. New York: Ballantine, 2001.

Otto, Rudolf. *The Idea of the Holy*. Trans. by John W. Harvey. Oxford University Press, 1923. I've omitted the overly lengthy subtitle.

Pascal, Blaise. *Pensées*. Translated, with an introduction, by A. J. Krailsheimer. Harmondsworth, UK: Penguin, 1966.

Potts, John. *A History of Charisma*. Palgrave Macmillan, 2009.

Read, Herbert. *The Forms of Things Unknown*. New York: Horizon Press, 1960. I had the privilege of meeting Sir Herbert when I was a college freshman in the early 1960s; he was very kind in complimenting the intelligence of a question that I put to him. I wish I could remember that question!

Roberts, Tim S. "The Even Harder Problem of Consciousness." *NeuroQuantology* 5 (2), September 2007, pp. 214-21. A somewhat nerdy article, but covers the topic ("Why am I me?").

Sacks, Oliver. *Musicophilia*. New York: Alfred A. Knopf, 2007. My wife is the proud possessor of a first edition, inscribed to her by the author.

_____. *The River of Consciousness*. New York: Vintage, 2017.

Sartre, Jean-Paul. *Nausea*. Trans. by Lloyd Alexander. The first English-language edition was published by New Directions in 1952 and a paperback edition appeared in 1959. I've misplaced a paperback edition that I had for many years; it had a nice introduction by Hayden Carruth. I've replaced it with a 2013 edition with an introduction by James Wood. I also have a paperback (Livres de Poche) edition in the original French. *La Nausée* was first published by Gallimard in 1938.

Scruton, Roger. *Kant*. Oxford University Press, 1982. Much of what I know of Kant's thought comes from this concise and readable book.

Searle, John R. *Mind, Brains and Science*. Cambridge, MA: Harvard University Press, 1986.

_____. *The Mystery of Consciousness*. New York Review, 1997.

_____. *The Rediscovery of the Mind*. Cambridge, MA: MIT Press, 1994.

Seth, Anil. *Being You: A New Science of Consciousness*. Dutton, 2021.

Smith, Huston. *The World's Religions*. New York: HarperCollins, 1991.

Solms, Mark. *The Hidden Spring: A Journey to the Source of Consciousness*. New York: W.W. Norton, 2021.

Tallis, Raymond. *Michelangelo's Finger: An Exploration of Everyday Transcendence*. New Haven: Yale University Press, 2010; London: Atlantic Books, 2010.

_____. *Seeing Ourselves: Reclaiming Humanity from God and Science*. Newcastle-upon-Tyne: Agenda, 2020.

_____. *Summers of Discontent: The Purpose of the Arts Today*. London: Wilmington Square Books, 2014.

Tillich, Paul. *The Courage to Be*. New Haven, CT: Yale University Press, 1952.

Unamuno, Miguel de. *Tragic Sense of Life*. Trans. by J. E. Crawford Flitch. New York: Dover, 1954.

Underhill, Evelyn. *Mysticism: A Study in the Nature and Development of Spiritual Consciousness*. E.P. Dutton, 1930; original edition published in 1911.

Watts, Alan W. *The Wisdom of Insecurity: A Message for an Age of Anxiety*. New York: Vintage Books, 1951.

Name Index

Alexander, Lloyd, 86

Allen, Woody, 63

Aquinas, Thomas, 63

Armstrong, Karen, 40, 41, 57, 58

Baars, Bernard, 16

Ball, Philip, 34-35

Bitbol, Michel, 1, 81

Blackmore, Susan, 19, 55

Boyer, Pascal, 85

Brinton, Howard, 45

Buber, Martin, xi, xii, 29, 31, 38, 51, 54, 58, 68, 74, 78

Butler, Samuel, 85

Calvin, William H., 36

Campbell, Joseph, 22, 29, 43, 54, 69, 71

Cassirer, Ernst, 42

Cézanne, Paul, 36

Chalmers, David, 10, 17

Copland, Aaron, 35

Corot, J.-B. Camille, 32

Crossan, John Dominic, 44, 69

Damasio, Antonio, 9, 13

Dante, 65

Darwin, Charles, 34, 35, 84

Dawkins, Richard, 81

Dehaene, Stanislas, 7, 16, 82

Dennett, Daniel, 11-12, 16, 80

Dutton, Denis, 31, 33, 34, 35

Eagleman, David, 6

Edelman, Gerald M., 13-14

Einstein, Albert, 1

Eiseley, Loren, 27, 28

Eliade, Mircea, 41, 42, 43, 57

Feinberg, Todd E., 83

Flynn, Thomas, x

Fodor, Jerry, 24

Frankl, Viktor, 22, 29

Freud, Sigmund, 27, 66

Friedman, Maurice, 90

Fromm, Erich, 28, 29, 40, 53

Galileo, 67

Gelernter, David, 8-9

Goff, Philip, 17

Gogh, Vincent van, 63

Graziano, Michael, 15-16

Harris, Annaka, 19

Harris, Sam, 19

Hart, George, 28

Heidegger, Martin, 16, 18, 60

Hesse, Hermann, 85

Hofstadter, Douglas, 2, 11, 16, 81

Holt, Jim, 2

Homer, 46, 65

Hood, Bruce, 19

Hume, David, 56

Humphrey, Nicholas, 9, 10, 24, 81

Iqbal, Muhammad, 54, 57

James, William, 68, 72

Jeffers, Robinson, 28, 40, 83

Jesus, 45-46, 70, 71

Job, 44, 75

Johnson, Steven, 56-57

Jones, Rufus, 73, 78

Judas Iscariot, 45

Jung, Carl G., 41, 43, 44, 52

Kafka, Franz, 63

Kandel, Eric, 35, 36
Kant, Immanuel, 5, 6, 8, 23, 32, 80
Kastrup, Bernardo, 18
Klaassen, Tim, 2-3
Kline, Franz, 33
Koch, Christof, 13
Krishnamurti, Jiddu, 54-56, 74, 85
Kuhn, Robert Lawrence, 80
Kuhn, Thomas, 22, 25
Lehrer, Jonah, 36
Leibniz, G. W., 8
Levinas, Emmanuel, 38
Levitin, Daniel, 33-34, 35
Lévy-Strauss, Claude, 23, 30, 43
Libet, Benjamin, 6
Louis, Morris, 32
Mallatt, Jon M., 83
Malraux, André, 65
Maritain, Jacques, 20-21
Martha (of Bethany), 45, 86
Mary (of Bethany), 45, 46
Maslow, Abraham, 22
Matisse, Henri, 32
Matthews, Eric, 29
McEwan, Ian, 10-11
McGinn, Colin, 10
Melville, Herman, 66
Merleau-Ponty, Maurice, 29
Metzinger, Thomas, 16
Michelangelo, 59
Mithen, Steven, 24-25, 27, 84
Mondrian, Piet, 36
Moore, Donald J., 86
Moses, 42, 68

Nagel, Thomas, 2, 4, 10, 62
Nearing, Helen, 64-65
Nearing, Scott, 64
Newberg, Andrew, 23, 33, 57
Nietzsche, Friedrich, 37
O'Gieblyn, Meghan, 82
Ortega y Gasset, José, 49, 77
Otto, Rudolf, xi, 27, 32-33, 41, 45, 51, 68, 72, 74
Pascal, Blaise, 1, 4, 10, 27, 61, 76, 78
Patel, Aniruddh, 34
Paul, Saint, 47-48, 61
Penrose, Roger, 16, 17, 82
Picasso, Pablo, 43
Pinker, Steven, 13, 34, 84
Potts, John, 47-48, 60
Read, Herbert, 38
Roberts, Tim S., 80
Sacks, Oliver, 12, 37, 84
Sargent, John Singer, 32
Sartre, Jean-Paul, xi, 5, 6, 38, 49, 50-52, 64, 69, 74-76, 79
Schopenhauer, Arthur, 80-81
Searle, John, 12
Seth, Anil, 14-16, 80
Shakespeare, William, 65
Smith, Huston, 54
Solms, Mark, 13-14, 16-17
Still, Clyfford, 32, 83
Stravinsky, Igor, 36
Tallis, Raymond, x, 6, 10, 25, 26, 27, 28-29, 37, 56, 59, 61, 78
Taves, Ann, 70-71
Tennyson, Alfred, Lord, 65, 88
Teresa of Ávila, Saint, 77, 86
Thomas, Dylan, 64
Tillich, Paul, 76

Tononi, Giulio, 15, 16
Tukaram, 54
Unamuno, Miguel de, 63, 77
Underhill, Evelyn, 68-70, 73-74
Watts, Alan, 54-56, 74
Weber, Max, 47
Wilson, Edward O., 27, 40
Yeats, William Butler, 57
Zuckerkandl, Victor, 37

IFF
BOOKS

ACADEMIC AND SPECIALIST

Iff Books publishes non-fiction. It aims to work with authors and titles that augment our understanding of the human condition, society and civilisation, and the world or universe in which we live. If you have enjoyed this book, why not tell other readers by posting a review on your preferred book site. Recent bestsellers from Iff Books are:

Why Materialism Is Baloney
How true skeptics know there is no death and fathom answers to life, the universe, and everything
Bernardo Kastrup
A hard-nosed, logical, and skeptic non-materialist metaphysics, according to which the body is in mind, not mind in the body.
Paperback: 978-1-78279-362-5 ebook: 978-1-78279-361-8

The Fall
Steve Taylor
The Fall discusses human achievement versus the issues of war, patriarchy and social inequality.
Paperback: 978-1-78535-804-3 ebook: 978-1-78535-805-0

Brief Peeks Beyond
Critical essays on metaphysics, neuroscience, free will, skepticism and culture
Bernardo Kastrup
An incisive, original, compelling alternative to current mainstream cultural views and assumptions.
Paperback: 978-1-78535-018-4 ebook: 978-1-78535-019-1

Framespotting
Changing how you look at things changes how you see them
Laurence & Alison Matthews
A punchy, upbeat guide to framespotting. Spot deceptions and hidden assumptions; swap growth for growing up. See and be free.
Paperback: 978-1-78279-689-3 ebook: 978-1-78279-822-4

Is There an Afterlife?
David Fontana
Is there an Afterlife? If so what is it like? How do Western ideas of the afterlife compare with Eastern? David Fontana presents the historical and contemporary evidence for survival of physical death.
Paperback: 978-1-90381-690-5

Nothing Matters
a book about nothing
Ronald Green
Thinking about Nothing opens the world to everything by illuminating new angles to old problems and stimulating new ways of thinking.
Paperback: 978-1-84694-707-0 ebook: 978-1-78099-016-3

Panpsychism
The Philosophy of the Sensuous Cosmos
Peter Ells
Are free will and mind chimeras? This book, anti-materialistic but respecting science, answers: No! Mind is foundational to all existence.
Paperback: 978-1-84694-505-2 ebook: 978-1-78099-018-7

Punk Science
Inside the Mind of God
Manjir Samanta-Laughton
Many have experienced unexplainable phenomena; God,
psychic abilities, extraordinary healing and angelic encounters.
Can cutting-edge science actually explain phenomena
previously thought of as 'paranormal'?
Paperback: 978-1-90504-793-2

The Vagabond Spirit of Poetry
Edward Clarke
Spend time with the wisest poets of the modern age and of the
past, and let Edward Clarke remind you of the importance of
poetry in our industrialized world.
Paperback: 978-1-78279-370-0 ebook: 978-1-78279-369-4

Readers of ebooks can buy or view any of these bestsellers by
clicking on the live link in the title. Most titles are published
in paperback and as an ebook. Paperbacks are available in
traditional bookshops. Both print and ebook formats are
available online. Find more titles and sign up to our readers'
newslett er at http://www.johnhuntpublishing.com/non-fiction
Follow us on Facebook at
https://www.facebook.com/JHPNonFiction
and Twitter at https://twitter.com/JHPNonFiction